CNN Short News for Listening
STEAM Education

Kazunori Kawasaki

JN099893

Asahi Press

音声再生アプリ「リスニング・トレーナー」を使った 音声ダウンロード

朝日出版社開発のアプリ、「リスニング・トレーナー（リストレ）」を使えば、教科書の音声を
スマホ、タブレットに簡単にダウンロードできます。どうぞご活用ください。

◉ アプリ【リスニング・トレーナー】の使い方

《アプリのダウンロード》

App Store または Google Play から
「リスニング・トレーナー」のアプリ
（無料）をダウンロード

App Storeは
こちら▶

Google Playは
こちら▶

《アプリの使い方》

① アプリを開き「コンテンツを追加」をタップ
② 画面上部に【15705】を入力し Done をタップ

音声・映像ストリーミング配信 ⟫⟫⟫

この教科書の音声及び、
付属の映像は、
右記ウェブサイトにて
無料で配信しています。

https://text.asahipress.com/free/english/

CNN Short News for Listening: STEAM Education

Copyright © 2023 by Asahi Press

All rights reserved. No part of this book may be reproduced or transmitted in any form or by any means, electronic or mechanical, including
photocopying, recording or by any information storage and retrieval system, without permission in writing from authors and the publisher.
CNN name, logo and all associated elements TM and © 2023 Cable News Network. A WarnerMedia Company. All rights reserved.

はじめに

　本書は、STEAM 教育の観点から短い英語ニュースを、世界最大のニュース専門メディア CNN 放送から選りすぐって収録したものです。1 本は、集中力を切らさず聞き通せる、30 秒ほどの長さになっています。

　音声は、CNN の放送そのものである「ナチュラル音声」のほか、ナレーターがゆっくり読み直した「ポーズ（無音の間）入り」と「ポーズなし」の音声が用意されています。これら 3 パターンの音声を使ってリスニング練習を行うと、世界標準のニュース英語がだれでも聞き取れるようになるはずです。[30 秒×3 回聞き]方式と本書が呼ぶこのリスニング練習には、通訳者養成学校でも採用されているサイトトランスレーションや区切り聞き、シャドーイングといった学習法が取り入れられているからです。

　巻頭に「3 つの効果的な学習法＋α」が説明されています。実際の練習に入る前に目を通しておくことをお勧めします。リスニング練習に加えて、TOEIC で問われるような主述の一致の理解も深めてみましょう。

　STEAM とは Science（科学）、Technology（技術）、Engineering（工学）、Arts（リベラルアーツ・芸術）、Mathematics（数学）の頭文字を組み合わせた教育概念です。STEAM 教育は、現在世界各国で導入され、日本でもAI 時代に対応するために推進されています。

　STEAM は、1990 年代からアメリカの幼稚園から高等学校（K-12）にいたる教育で注目され推進された STEM 教育にヤークマン（2006、2008）が Arts を加えたもので、この教育で、総合教育カリキュラムを提唱しました。Arts を加えたのは、Arts の領域が知識や幅広い教養を持った人間の総体的な教育に重要であると認識したためでした。Arts は、芸術（art）と解されたりもしますが、本書ではヤークマンに倣いリベラルアーツと捉えています。科学と技術は工学とリベラルアーツを介して理解され、すべて数学的要因に基づいているとヤークマンは主張しています。科学、技術、工学、リベラルアーツ、数学といった学問・専門分野の文理横断の概念を理解することで、それらの現実世界への適用方法を学ぶと共に、自分自身の現実世界への適応方法を学ぶ原動力にもなります。

　本書で扱うニュースを題材として、どのように学問領域が現実に互いに結びついているか再考し、英語で語り合ってみてください。

2022 年 10 月

川﨑　和基

CONTENTS

● How to Get the MP3 and Video Data ———————————— 02

● Introduction ————————————————————————— 03

● How to use the text book ————————————————— 06

● How to Improve Your English Skills ————————————— 08

[Unit 1] **A Robot That Can Do Backflips** ———— Track 02-03-04-48 13

[Unit 2] **Bringing Back the Mammoth** ———— Track 05-06-07-49 17

[Unit 3] **High-Tech Implants for the Brain** ———— Track 08-09-10-50 21

[Unit 4] **Unique Bridge in Vietnam** ———— Track 11-12-13-51 25

[Unit 5] **On the Hunt with Pokémon Go** ———— Track 14-15-16-52 29

[Unit 6] **Beetle Gives Hints on Toughness** ———— Track 17-18-19-53 33

[Unit 7] **Successful Test of Flying Car** ———— Track 20-21-22-54 37

[Unit 8] **Quadriplegic Uses Brain Tech to Walk** ———— Track 23-24-25-55 41

[Unit 9] **Google Maps Gets Ecofriendly** ———— Track 26-27-28-56 45

[Unit 10] **Stone Age Musical Instrument** ———— Track 29-30-31-57 49

[Unit 11] **Concerts Staged by Hologram** ———— Track 32-33-34-58 53

[Unit 12] **A Selfie in Your Coffee** ———— Track 35-36-37-59 57

[Unit 13] **World's Largest Water Gun** ———— Track 38-39-40-60 61

[Unit 14] **FDA Approves 3D-Printed Pill** ———— Track 41-42-43-61 65

[Unit 15] **USA Beats Japan in Robot Fight** ———— Track 44-45-46-62 69

[Reading] **No Basis for Bias** ———— Track 63-64-65-66 74

目次

●音声・映像再生ガイド ——————————— 02

●はじめに ———————————————— 03

●本書の使い方 ————————————— 06

●3つの効果的な学習法＋α ———————— 08

| Unit 1 | 米企業がバク宙する人型ロボットを開発 ——————— Track 02-03-04-48 | 13 |

| Unit 2 | DNA を使用したマンモス復活計画が始動 !? ——————— Track 05-06-07-49 | 17 |

| Unit 3 | イーロン・マスク、「脳と AI の融合」を目指す ————— Track 08-09-10-50 | 21 |

| Unit 4 | 巨人の両手が支える橋がベトナムの新名所に ————— Track 11-12-13-51 | 25 |

| Unit 5 | ポケモン GO が現実社会を変える？ ———————— Track 14-15-16-52 | 29 |

| Unit 6 | 車にひかれても平気！頑丈すぎる甲虫の謎に挑む ——— Track 17-18-19-53 | 33 |

| Unit 7 | 日本企業による「空飛ぶ車」の実用化が間近 !? ————— Track 20-21-22-54 | 37 |

| Unit 8 | 四肢まひの患者に光、脳信号で「手足」操作 ————— Track 23-24-25-55 | 41 |

| Unit 9 | Google マップに新機能！エコフレンドリーなルートとは？ — Track 26-27-28-56 | 45 |

| Unit 10 | 1万8000年前！よみがえる石器時代の楽器の音色 —— Track 29-30-31-57 | 49 |

| Unit 11 | ホログラム技術、コロナ禍のライブ業界を救う !? ——— Track 32-33-34-58 | 53 |

| Unit 12 | 自撮り画像のコーヒーアートでインスタ映え ————— Track 35-36-37-59 | 57 |

| Unit 13 | 元 NASA 技術者が「世界最強の水鉄砲」を開発 ———— Track 38-39-40-60 | 61 |

| Unit 14 | 3D プリンターで製造した薬を米当局が初認可 ———— Track 41-42-43-61 | 65 |

| Unit 15 | リアル巨大ロボット、日米大決戦！———————— Track 44-45-46-62 | 69 |

| Reading | 「女子は数学が不得意」は誤り
計算中の脳の活動は男女で同等と判明 ———— Track 63-64-65-66 | 74 |

本書の使い方

1ページ目で、英語のみでキーワードとキーフレーズを利用してニュースの内容を理解してみましょう。2ページ目で、日本語の語注とトランスクリプトを利用して、ニュースの内容を理解してみましょう。3ページ目で、「3つの効果的な学習法＋α」を利用して学習しましょう。4ページ目で、STEAMに基づき、ニュースの内容を理解し、さらに関連した技術や研究開発に興味をもってみましょう。

（1ページ目）

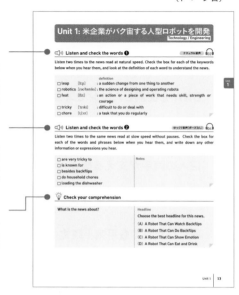

●Listen and check the words ❶

2回ナチュラル音声を聞いて、ニュースの内容理解に必要なキーワードとなる5つの単語を聞き取れた時に、□にチェックを入れてみてください。そして、それぞれの単語の定義を参考にしながら、英語のみで内容を理解してみましょう。

●Listen and check the words ❷

2回ポーズが入っていないゆっくり音声を聞いて、ニュースの内容理解に必要なキーフレーズ（語句）を聞き取れた時に、□にチェックを入れてみてください。そして、それぞれのキーフレーズの前後に聞き取れた語句を加えて、さらに内容理解を深めましょう。

●Check your comprehension

キーワードやキーフレーズならびにその前後のフレーズを聞き取った後、ニュースの内容を書いてみましょう。内容理解を深めた後、ニュースのタイトルにふさわしいものを選んでみましょう。

（2ページ目）

●Transcript

トランスクリプトを見ながら、ナチュラル音声やゆっくり音声を聞いて、1ページ目で理解した内容と合っているか確かめてみてください。そして、さらにニュースの内容理解を深めてみましょう。

●TOEIC-style Questions

ニュースの内容理解を確認するために、TOEIC形式の問題に挑戦してみましょう。

● Transcript divided by slashes

「3つの効果的な学習法＋α」にある①速読能力が高まるサイトトランスレーション、②速聴能力が高まる区切り聞き、③総合力を養うシャドーイング、④主述の一致の英語学習法を利用してみましょう。

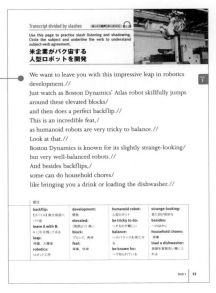

Transcript divided by slashes 〈ゆっくり音声[ポーズ入り]〉

Use this page to practice slash listening and shadowing. Circle the subject and underline the verb to understand subject-verb agreement.

米企業がバク宙する人型ロボットを開発

We want to leave you with this impressive leap in robotics development.//
Just watch as Boston Dynamics' Atlas robot skillfully jumps around these elevated blocks/
and then does a perfect backflip.//
This is an incredible feat,/
as humanoid robots are very tricky to balance.//
Look at that.//
Boston Dynamics is known for its slightly strange-looking/
but very well-balanced robots.//
And besides backflips,/
some can do household chores/
like bringing you a drink or loading the dishwasher.//

語注

backflip:〈タイトル〉後方宙返り、バク宙	**development:**開発	**humanoid robot:**人型ロボット	**strange-looking:**見た目が奇妙な
leave A with B:AにBを残しておる	**elevated:**（周囲より）高い	**be tricky to do:**〜するのが難しい	**besides:**〜のほかに
leap:飛躍、大躍進	**block:**ブロック、角材	**balance:**〜のバランスを保たせる	**household chores:**家事
robotics:ロボット工学	**feat:**偉業、快挙	**be known for:**〜で知られている	**load a dishwasher:**食器洗い機に入れる

Unit 1　15

● ニュースのミニ知識

ニュースで取り上げられている内容をさらに理解できるように情報を加えています。

（4ページ目）

■ ナチュラル音声のアクセント

アメリカ英語

■ ニュースのミニ知識

ボストン ダイナミクスは、1992年にマサチューセッツ工科大学のマーク・レイバートと彼の同僚たちにより設立された。同社はアメリカ国防高等研究計画局の支援の下、四足歩行ロボットの開発に携わっていた。ビッグドッグといった4足歩行ロボットの開発から、最近では、スポットといった地形を読み取り、機能に障害物を避け、通り抜ける建設現場での使用を目的としたロボットや、ストレッチといった倉庫や物流会社で積み降ろし入れするロボットの販売に至っている。アトラスは2017年にはバク宙するまでになり、その後改良が進み、コンパクトな世界最小の油圧駆動力ユニットを持ち、3Dプリンターで作られたパーツを使い、重さ85kgで障害物を走り回ったり、走る・跳ぶ・登るといったパルクールをやってのけるまでになる。

■ Technology / Engineering のミニ知識

大手系チェーンでは、ロボットが出迎えてくれたり、食事の配膳をしてくれたり、また、工場等では産業用ロボットが使われるというようにロボットは身近なものとなっている。ロボットの開発には機械工学、電気電子工学、情報工学、電子制御の様々な技術が必要となる。ロボットはプログラム通りに行動するため、仮想空間にはない障害が現実にはあるため、その障害を自ら認識し回避するための制御アルゴリズムや、開閉に用いる油圧技術の改良など、多くの研究課題がある。今後、自然災害や事故などで活躍するロボットの開発が期待される。

Words & Phrases （ロボットに関する研究開発や産業などに関連した言葉）

☐ research and development (R&D)　☐ 研究開発
☐ industrial robot　☐ 産業用ロボット
☐ medical robot　☐ 医療用ロボット
☐ rescue robot　☐ 救助ロボット
☐ robotic arm　☐ ロボットアーム
☐ control system　☐ 制御装置
☐ hydraulic power unit　☐ 油圧パワーユニット
☐ control algorithm　☐ 制御アルゴリズム
☐ automated work　☐ 自動作業
☐ unloading　☐ 荷下ろし

■ Let's Think!

ロボットに関わる身近な技術や研究開発を調べて、英語（難しければ日本語で）まとめよう。

16　STEAM教育

● Science/Technology/Engineering/Arts/Mathmatics のミニ知識

ニュースにある内容は学際的な研究が統合して実現しています。ここでは、STEAM教育で提唱されている、Science, Technology, Engineering, Arts, Mathematics の中で、ニュースで取り上げられている内容と特に関連した分野を紹介しています。それぞれの分野は、今後研究開発が期待されているものです。将来の研究課題のヒントにしてみてください。STEAM教育では、Mathematics は、Science, Technology, Engineering, Arts を理解する基底となるものであるため、すべてのニュースの内容に関連しています。従って、Science, Technology, Engineering, Arts を関連分野として取り上げていますが、Mathematics が含まれていると理解してください。

● Words & Phrases

STEAM教育に基づきニュースの内容に関連や発展させた語句を記載しています。ここに記載されている語句を手がかりとして専門的かつ学際的な研究に興味をもってみましょう。

● Let's Think!

STEAMを意識して、ニュースの内容に関連や発展させた身近な技術や研究開発を調べて、英語あるいは日本語でまとめてみましょう。

3つの効果的な学習法＋α

　本書は「30秒×3回聞き」方式を採用しています。これによって、だれでも世界標準の英語ニュースが聞き取れるようになるはずです。

　「30秒×3回聞き」方式とは、30秒という集中力が途切れない長さのニュースを、3種類の音声で聞くというものです。そのため、ご提供する音声（音声の入手・再生方法については p.2 を参照）は、各ニュースが「ナチュラル音声」、「ゆっくり音声（ポーズ入り）」、「ゆっくり音声（ポーズなし）」という3種類で収録されています。また、文字としてもそれらに対応する形の英文が掲載されています。

　これらの音声や英文は、ただ単に聞いたり読んだりするのではなく、以下に示すサイトトランスレーション、区切り聞き、シャドーイングという3つの学習法と結びつけることで高い効果を生むようになっています。

❶速読能力が高まるサイトトランスレーション

　俗に「サイトラ」と呼ばれます。英語でつづると sight translation です。sight は、名詞として「視力、視覚」、形容詞として「見てすぐの、初見での」という意味を持ちます。目にしたところからすぐに訳していくのが sight translation です。

　サイトラの練習では、英文を頭から語順通りに目で追い、情報・意味の区切り目と思われる個所にスラッシュ（／）を書き入れ、区切られた部分をすぐに訳します。それを英文の最後まで次々と繰り返すのですが、こうした訳し方を「順送りの訳」と呼ぶこともあります。

　なお、英文をどのくらい細かく区切るか、どこを情報・意味の区切り目としてスラッシュを入れるかは人それぞれでよく、絶対的なルールがあるわけではありません。

利点・効能　サイトラを行うと、書かれた英文がその語順通りに理解できるようになり、自然と「速読」に結びつきます。そして、英文を素早く理解できるようになるということは、英文を英文としてそのまま理解できるということにつながっていきます。また、「読んで分からないものは聞いても分からない」という原則に従えば、サイトラの速読能力が「区切り聞き」で養う速聴能力の土台になるといえます。

本書での学習法　本書では、各ニュースの放送音声を文字に書き起こし、普通の英文

(transcript) とスラッシュで区切られた英文(transcript divided by slashes) の形で掲載しています。まずはスラッシュで区切られた英文を順番にどんどん訳していく練習をしましょう。

本書で示されたスラッシュの入れ方はあくまで一例です。これに従ってしばらく練習しているとサイトラのやり方が感覚的につかめてきますので、やり方が分かったら、普通の英文を自分なりの区切り方で訳してみると、よい練習になります。

練習のポイント サイトラはなるべく素早く行うことが大切です。英文は「読んだ端から消えていくもの」くらいに考えて、次々と順送りの訳をこなしていきましょう。そうしているうちに読むスピードが速くなるはずですし、区切り聞きにもつながります。

❷速聴能力が高まる区切り聞き

サイトラをリスニングのトレーニングに応用したのが、「区切り聞き」と呼ばれる学習法です。サイトラでは英語が目から入ってきましたが、区切り聞きでは英語が耳から入ってくることになります。

区切り聞きの場合、英文にスラッシュを入れる代わりに、情報・意味の区切り目と思われる個所でオーディオプレーヤーを一時停止させ、すぐに訳します。その部分を訳し終えたら再び音声を先に進め、同様の作業を繰り返していきます。

利点・効能 区切り聞きを行うと、話された英文がその語順通りに理解できるようになり、自然と「速聴」に結びつきます。そして、英文を素早く理解できるようになるということは、英文を英文としてそのまま理解できるということにつながっていきます。

本書での学習法 だれでも英語ニュースが聞き取れるようになるよう、本書では区切り聞き練習を重視しています。ご提供する音声に収録されている「ゆっくり音声(ポーズ入り)」を利用することで、オーディオプレーヤーを自分でいちいち一時停止させる面倒がなくなり、区切り聞きがしやすくなっています。ポーズ(無音の間)の位置はサイトラのスラッシュと同じにしてありますが、ポーズで区切られた部分を素早く訳していきましょう。

音声には、各ニュースが「ナチュラル音声」、「ゆっくり音声（ポーズ入り）」、「ゆっくり音声（ポーズなし）」の順番で入っています。まずは「ナチュラル音声」を聞いて全体の内容を推測し、次に「ゆっくり音声（ポーズ入り）」を使った区切り聞きで部分ごとに順番に理解できるようになり、その後「ゆっくり音声（ポーズなし）」で全体を頭から素早く理解していくことができるかどうか試してみてください。

なお、最後には、全ニュースのナチュラル音声だけを集めて、もう一度収録してあります。これらを頭から素早く理解していけるようになるのが最終目標です。

練習のポイント 音声は流れる端から消えていってしまいます。英文を後ろから前に戻って理解するなどということはできないため、耳に入った文を瞬時に理解する英語力と集中力が求められます。このトレーニングによってリスニング力は必ず向上するので、集中力を高める訓練をするつもりで挑戦してみましょう。

特にニュースを聞く場合、背景知識があると情報がすんなりと頭に入りますから、日ごろからいろいろな記事について興味を持っておくことも大切です。本書には「ニュースのミニ知識」が掲載されているので、役立ててください。

英文は論理的と言われますが、特にニュースでは、全体の起承転結の流れはもちろん、ひとつのセンテンスの中でも、「①だれ（何）が ②だれ（何）に対して ③何を ④いつ ⑤どこで」という情報がかなり秩序だって含まれています。このような情報を意識して聞くと、リスニングも楽になります。

❸総合力を養うシャドーイング

シャドーイングは英語でshadowingとつづります。shadowという語には動詞として「影のように付いていく」という意味がありますが、学習法としてのシャドーイングは、聞こえてくる英語音声を一歩後から追いかけるようにリピートしていくものです。オリジナルの英語音声に遅れないように付いていく様子が「影」のようなので、こう名づけられました。

利点・効能 シャドーイングは、今聞いた音声をリピートしながら、同時に次の音声のリスニングも行うというものなので、アウトプットとインプットの同時進行になります。その

ため同時通訳のトレーニングとして普及しましたが、一般の英語学習者にも有益であることがいろいろな研究で認められています。

　通常のリスニング練習は学習者が音声を聞くだけ、すなわち受動的なやり方であるのに対し、シャドーイングは学習者の参加を伴うもの、いわば能動的な学習法です。この能動的な学習法は、受動的なものに比べ、よりいっそう集中力を高める訓練になり、リスニング力を向上させます。また、正しい発音やイントネーションを身につける訓練にもなり、ひいてはスピーキング力を高めるのにも役立ちます。

　本書での学習法　シャドーイングは難易度の高い学習法なので、「ナチュラル音声」でいきなり練習するのではなく、最初は「ゆっくり音声（ポーズなし）」を利用するのがよいでしょう。それでも難しいと感じる人も多いでしょうから、「ゆっくり音声（ポーズ入り）」から始めるのも一案です。ポーズが入った音声を用いるのは本来のシャドーイングとは違うという考え方もありますが、無理をして挫折することのないよう、まずはできることから始めてください。

　練習のポイント　シャドーイングでは、流れてくる音声を一字一句リピートしなければならないため、ひとつひとつの単語に神経を集中するあまり、文全体の意味を把握できなくなることがよくあります。きちんと論旨を追いながらトレーニングすることが大切です。

　ただし、区切り聞きのように日本語に順次訳していこうと思ってはいけません。英語を正確に聞き取り、正確な発音とイントネーションでリピートしようとしているときに、頭の中に日本語を思い浮かべていては混乱するだけだからです。シャドーイングには、区切り聞きから一歩進んで、英語を英語のまま理解する力が必要になってきます。

　もしも英語でのシャドーイングがどうしても難しすぎるという場合は、まず日本語でシャドーイングする練習から始めてみましょう。

＋α（プラスアルファ）の学習法

◆主述の一致

　主語と述語動詞を一致させる問題はTOEICでよく出題されます。主語の人称（1人称、2人称、3人称）や数（単数・複数）によって、be動詞・一般動詞の現在形やbe動詞の過去形など適切なものを選ばなければなりません。また、接続詞で結ばれた複合主語もあり、複数ある主語のうちどの主語に述語動詞を一致させるかにも注意しなければなりません。

　主語となる名詞には○印を、動詞には下線を引くなどして、主述が一致していることを確かめてみてください。

　利点・効果　TOEICやTOEFL ITPなどの主述の一致問題の対策にもなります。また、主述の一致を意識することで、会話や英作文といった英語使用のアウトプットの際に役立つことにもなります。

　本書での学習法　主語となる名詞と一致させる動詞を探しながら、品詞を理解することで文構造が見えてきます。速読をした後、品詞を理解しながら語注を参考にして精読にも挑戦してみましょう。さらに、各UnitにあるTOEIC形式の問題にも挑戦してみてください。

　学習のポイント　文の要素として、主語となるのは複数の語で形成される主部（名詞句）や主部のなかで中心となる語（名詞）です。まずは、主部を見つけ、次に主部のなかで中心となる語（名詞）を探してみましょう。次に、述語動詞を探し、主語の人称や数と一致しているか確認してみてください。主語には、複合主語や省略もありますので注意してください。

Unit 1: 米企業がバク宙する人型ロボットを開発

Listen and check the words ❶

ナチュラル音声 02

Listen two times to the news read at natural speed. Check the box for each of the keywords below when you hear them, and look at the definition of each word to understand the news.

		definition
☐ leap	[liːp]	: a sudden change from one thing to another
☐ robotics	[rəʊ'bɒtɪks]	: the science of designing and operating robots
☐ feat	[fiːt]	: an action or a piece of work that needs skill, strength or courage
☐ tricky	['trɪki]	: difficult to do or deal with
☐ chore	[tʃɔːr]	: a task that you do regularly

Listen and check the words ❷

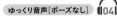 ゆっくり音声[ポーズなし] 04

Listen two times to the same news read at slow speed without pauses. Check the box for each of the words and phrases below when you hear them, and write down any other information or expressions you hear.

☐ are very tricky to
☐ is known for
☐ besides backflips
☐ do household chores
☐ loading the dishwasher

Notes

Check your comprehension

What is the news about?

Headline

Choose the best headline for this news.

(A) A Robot That Can Watch Backflips

(B) A Robot That Can Do Backflips

(C) A Robot That Can Show Emotion

(D) A Robot That Can Eat and Drink

Check the transcript and make sure you understand the content. Then listen to the news again and again until you can catch all of it.

A Robot That Can Do Backflips

We want to leave you with this impressive leap in robotics development. Just watch as Boston Dynamics' Atlas robot skillfully jumps around these elevated blocks and then does a perfect backflip. This is an incredible feat, as humanoid robots are very tricky to balance. Look at that. Boston Dynamics is known for its slightly strange-looking but very well-balanced robots. And besides backflips, some can do household chores like bringing you a drink or loading the dishwasher.

Aired on November 17, 2017

TOEIC-style Questions

1. What is the Atlas robot's most impressive ability?

(A) Its ability to deliver drinks

(B) Its ability to load a dishwasher

(C) Its ability to manipulate blocks

(D) Its ability to do a backflip

2. What is probably the biggest challenge in achieving what the anchor calls an incredible feat?

(A) Staying well-balanced

(B) Using strength without breaking anything

(C) Avoiding the elevated blocks

(D) Jumping onto the elevated blocks

Transcript divided by slashes

ゆっくり音声［ポーズ入り］ 03

Use this page to practice slash listening and shadowing. Circle the subject and underline the verb to understand subject-verb agreement.

米企業がバク宙する
人型ロボットを開発

We want to leave you with this impressive leap in robotics development.//

Just watch as Boston Dynamics' Atlas robot skillfully jumps around these elevated blocks/

and then does a perfect backflip.//

This is an incredible feat,/

as humanoid robots are very tricky to balance.//

Look at that.//

Boston Dynamics is known for its slightly strange-looking/

but very well-balanced robots.//

And besides backflips,/

some can do household chores/

like bringing you a drink or loading the dishwasher.//

語注

backflip:《タイトル》後方宙返り、バク宙	**development:** 開発	**humanoid robot:** 人型ロボット	**strange-looking:** 見た目が奇妙な
leave A with B: A に B を残して去る	**elevated:**（周囲より）高い	**be tricky to do:** ～するのが難しい	**besides:** ～のほかに
leap: 飛躍、大躍進	**block:** ブロック、角材	**balance:** ～のバランスを保たせる	**household chores:** 家事
robotics: ロボット工学	**feat:** 偉業、快挙	**be known for:** ～で知られている	**load a dishwasher:** 食器を食器洗い機に入れる

■ ナチュラル音声のアクセント

アメリカ英語

■ ニュースのミニ知識

ボストン・ダイナミクスは、1992年にマサチューセッツ工科大学のマーク・レイバートと彼の同僚たちにより設立された。同社はアメリカ国防高等研究計画局の支援の下、四足歩行ロボットの開発に携わっていた。ビックドックといった4足歩行ロボットの開発から、最近では、スポットという地形を読み取り、機敏に障害物を避け、通り抜ける建設現場等での使用を目的としたロボットや、ストレッチといった倉庫や運送会社で積み荷を出し入れするロボットの販売に至っている。アトラスは2017年にはバク宙をしてみせたが、その後改良が進み、コンパクトな世界最小の油圧装置と油圧動力ユニットを持ち、3Dプリンターで作られたパーツを使い、重さ85kgで障害物を走り抜けたり、走る・跳ぶ・登るといったパルクールをやってのけるまでになる。

■ Technology / Engineering のミニ知識

大手外食チェーンでは、ロボットが出迎えてくれたり、食事の配膳をしてくれたり、また、工場等では産業用ロボットが使われるというようにロボットは身近なものとなっている。ロボットの開発には機械工学、電気電子工学、情報工学、電子制御、計測制御などの様々な技術を必要とする。ロボットはプログラム通りに行動する一方、仮想空間にはない障害が現実にはあるため、その障害を自ら認識し回避するための制御アルゴリズムや、関節に用いる油圧技術の改良など、多くの研究課題がある。今後、自然災害や事故などでも活躍するロボットの開発が期待される。

Words & Phrases （ロボットに関する研究開発や産業などに関連した言葉）

☐ research and development（R&D）	☐ 研究開発
☐ industrial robot	☐ 産業用ロボット
☐ medical robot	☐ 医療用ロボット
☐ rescue robot	☐ 救助ロボット
☐ robotic arm	☐ ロボットアーム
☐ control system	☐ 制御装置
☐ hydraulic power unit	☐ 油圧パワーユニット
☐ control algorithm	☐ 制御アルゴリズム
☐ automated work	☐ 自動作業
☐ unloading	☐ 荷下ろし

■ Let's Think!

ロボットに関わる身近な技術や研究開発を調べて、英語で（難しければ日本語で）まとめてみよう。

Science / Technology

 Listen and check the words ❶

ナチュラル音声 05

Listen two times to the news read at natural speed. Check the box for each of the keywords below when you hear them, and look at the definition of each word to understand the news.

		definition
☐ roam	[rəʊm]	: to walk or travel around an area without any definite aim or direction
☐ bioscience	[ˈbaɪəʊsaɪəns]	: any of the life sciences
☐ genetics	[dʒəˈnetɪks]	: the scientific study of the ways in which different characteristics are passed from each generation of living things to the next
☐ resurrect	[ˌrezəˈrekt]	: to bring a dead person back to life
☐ proponent	[prəˈpəʊnənt]	: a person who supports an idea or course of action

Unit 2

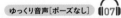 **Listen and check the words ❷**

ゆっくり音声[ポーズなし] 07

Listen two times to the same news read at slow speed without pauses. Check the box for each of the words and phrases below when you hear them, and write down any other information or expressions you hear.

	Notes
☐ once again	
☐ has raised $15 million	
☐ plan to use DNA	
☐ in an altered form	
☐ in fighting the climate crisis	

 Check your comprehension

What is the news about?

Headline

Choose the best headline for this news.

（A） Elephants Roaming the Earth

（B） Visiting the Prehistoric Monument

（C） Bringing Back the Mammoth

（D） Survival in Arctic Tundra

Check the transcript and make sure you understand the content. Then listen to the news again and again until you can catch all of it.

Bringing Back the Mammoth

Woolly mammoths may soon roam the earth once again. A new biosciences and genetics company named Colossal has raised $15 million to resurrect the prehistoric creature. They plan to use DNA extracted from a mammoth's frozen remains, mixed with elephant DNA, to create an enormous elephant-mammoth hybrid. Proponents say bringing back the mammoth in an altered form would be useful in fighting the climate crisis and help to restore the fragile Arctic tundra ecosystem.

Aired on September 15, 2021

TOEIC-style Questions

1. How much money has been raised for this project?
   (A) $6 million
   (B) $15 million
   (C) $50 million
   (D) $60 million

2. According to this news report, what is one reason for bringing back the woolly mammoth?
   (A) To learn more about DNA
   (B) To help restore an ecosystem
   (C) To provide a new source of food
   (D) To help elephants live longer

Use this page to practice slash listening and shadowing. Circle the subject and underline the verb to understand subject-verb agreement.

DNA を使用した
マンモス復活計画が始動！？

COLOSSAL ENDEAVOR
SCIENTISTS GET $15 MILLION TO RESURRECT WOO
CEIVED "CREDIBLE ALLEGATIONS" OF REPRISAL KILLINGS O

Unit 2

Woolly mammoths may soon roam the earth once again.//

A new biosciences and genetics company named Colossal/

has raised $15 million/

to resurrect the prehistoric creature.//

They plan to use DNA extracted from a mammoth's frozen remains,/

mixed with elephant DNA,/

to create an enormous elephant-mammoth hybrid.//

Proponents say/

bringing back the mammoth in an altered form/

would be useful in fighting the climate crisis/

and help to restore the fragile Arctic tundra ecosystem.//

語注

woolly mammoth: ケナガマンモス	**resurrect:** 〜を生き返らせる、よみがえらせる	**hybrid:** 交配種、雑種	**restore:** 〜を元の状態に戻す、回復させる
roam: 〜を歩き回る、うろつく	**prehistoric:** 有史以前の、先史時代の	**proponent:** 提案者、支持者	**fragile:** 壊れやすい、もろい
bioscience: 生物科学、生命科学	**extract A from B:** AをBから抽出する	**altered:** 改変された、変更された	**Arctic:** 北極の、北極圏の
genetics: 遺伝学	**remains:** 遺骸、死骸	**climate crisis:** 気候危機	**tundra:** 凍土帯、ツンドラ

■ ナチュラル音声のアクセント

オーストラリア英語

■ ニュースのミニ知識

ハーバード大学医学部教授のジョージ・チャーチ氏が起業家ベン・ラム氏と共同で設立したコロッサル社は、2021年9月、1500万ドルの資金を基にマンモスを復活させる計画を発表した。コロッサル社は、ケナガマンモスの寒さに強いゲノムの優位形質の解明をしながら、遺伝子科学と気候変動の繋がりを検証し、マンモスの復活が地球保護に繋がると考え、現存する象を絶滅から救うばかりか、永久凍土層に閉じ込められている温室効果ガスの噴出の抑制や、北極の低木で覆われた森林を大草原に変えて、二酸化炭素排出対策への寄与を含む10の目標を掲げている。

■ Science / Technology のミニ知識

農学の分野で、気候変動に対応する作物育種と遺伝育種研究が行われ、作物のゲノム育種技術の開発が進められている。また、ゲノム解析やその情報を利用して、遺伝子に手を加え、気候変動にも適用できる生命を作り出そうとしている。温室効果ガス排出の90％以上を吸収する海で生息する珊瑚は、気候変動の影響を受け、年々珊瑚礁の消滅範囲が広がっているが、遺伝子技術がその減少に歯止めをかけるかもしれない。一方で、遺伝子操作による負の影響も考えられ、変異した動植物が自然界に予期せぬ結果をもたらすこともある。遺伝子についての研究は、生物学や医学の分野ばかりではなく、気候変動などにも関わる幅広い分野で応用されている。

Words & Phrases（遺伝子や気候変動に関する研究開発や産業などに関連した言葉）

- □ genetics　　　　　　　　　　　　　　□ 遺伝学
- □ genetic engineering　　　　　　　　　□ 遺伝子工学
- □ genome　　　　　　　　　　　　　　 □ ゲノム
- □ genetic code　　　　　　　　　　　　□ 遺伝暗号
- □ genetically modified foods　　　　　　□ 遺伝子組み換え食品
- □ breeding　　　　　　　　　　　　　　□ 品種改良
- □ climate change　　　　　　　　　　　□ 気候変動
- □ greenhouse gas emission　　　　　　　□ 温室効果ガス排出
- □ global warming　　　　　　　　　　　□ 地球温暖化
- □ Intergovernmental Panel on Climate Change（IPCC）　□ 気候変動に関する政府間パネル

■ Let's Think!

遺伝子に関する身近な技術や研究開発を調べて、英語で（難しければ日本語で）まとめてみよう。

🔊 Listen and check the words ❶

ナチュラル音声 08

Listen two times to the news read at natural speed. Check the box for each of the keywords below when you hear them, and look at the definition of each word to understand the news.

		definition
☐ merge	[mɜːdʒ]	: to combine or make two or more things combine to form a single thing
☐ implant	[ɪmˈplɑːnt]	: to put something into a part of the body, usually in a medical operation
☐ device	[dɪˈvaɪs]	: an object or a piece of equipment that has been designed to do a particular job
☐ cognitive	[ˈkɑɡnətɪv]	: connected with mental processes of understanding
☐ defect	[ˈdíːfekt]	: a fault in something or in the way it has been made that means that it is not perfect

Unit 3

🔊 Listen and check the words ❷

ゆっくり音声[ポーズなし] 10

Listen two times to the same news read at slow speed without pauses. Check the box for each of the words and phrases below when you hear them, and write down any other information or expressions you hear.

	Notes
☐ aims to implant	
☐ as well	
☐ by the end of	
☐ are warning about	
☐ gaining access to	

 ## Check your comprehension

What is the news about?	Headline
	Choose the best headline for this news.
	(A) The Improvement of Computer Memory
	(B) Computers and iPhone App
	(C) The Risks of Motor Business
	(D) High-Tech Implants for the Brain

Check the transcript and make sure you understand the content. Then listen to the news again and again until you can catch all of it.

High-Tech Implants for the Brain

SpaceX founder Elon Musk's latest vision for the future is a way to merge your brain with artificial intelligence. Musk is cofounder of Neuralink, a start-up which aims to implant a device in the brain that would communicate with an iPhone app and computers as well. Musk says the device could be used to improve memory, repair motor function or just help people with cognitive defects. He says the trials could begin by the end of next year. Critics, though, are warning about the risks of business enterprises gaining access to brain data.

Aired on July 18, 2019

TOEIC-style Questions

1. What does Neuralink hope to do?

(A) Link people's brains to artificial intelligence

(B) Develop computer memory

(C) Explore space

(D) Connect iPhones with computers

2. Who is likely to be especially interested in using this device?

(A) Someone who wants to learn about outer space

(B) Someone with a cognitive problem

(C) Someone who needs their iPhone repaired

(D) Someone with extremely high intelligence

Use this page to practice slash listening and shadowing. Circle the subject and underline the verb to understand subject-verb agreement.

イーロン・マスク、
「脳とAIの融合」を目指す

ECTING WITH AI

LOOKING TO IMPLANT CHIPS IN HUMAN BRAIN

Unit
3

SpaceX founder Elon Musk's latest vision for the future/

is a way to merge your brain with artificial intelligence.//

Musk is cofounder of Neuralink,/

a start-up which aims to implant a device in the brain/

that would communicate with an iPhone app and computers as well.//

Musk says/

the device could be used to improve memory, repair motor function/

or just help people with cognitive defects.//

He says/

the trials could begin by the end of next year.//

Critics, though, are warning about the risks/

of business enterprises gaining access to brain data.//

語注

implant:《タイトル》①移植、移植物 ②～を移植する	**artificial intelligence:** 人工知能、AI	**improve:** ～を改善する、向上する	**critic:** 批判する人
founder: 創設者、創立者	**start-up:** 新興企業	**repair:** ～を直す、修復する	**warn about:** ～について警告する
merge A with B: AとBを融合する、同化させる	**aim to do:** ～することを目指す	**motor function:** 運動機能	**business enterprise:** 企業、事業
	device: 機器、装置	**cognitive defect:** 認知障害	**gain access to:** ～にアクセスする

■ ナチュラル音声のアクセント

オーストラリア英語

■ ニュースのミニ知識

頭の中で考えるだけで様々なものを動かしたり、麻痺している体が動くようになったらどうであろうか。ニューラリンク社の共同創業者兼CEOでもあるマスク氏は、2020年夏にその事業について説明した。人間の脳の860億もの神経細胞は互いに繋がり、シナプスを介して様々な電気信号を送受信する。神経細胞の近くに電極を入れ、神経細胞から得られる生体情報を記録し、解読すれば、コンピューターやスマホなどを、手を触れずに使えるであろう。このような試みから「リンク（Link）」が開発された。2021年4月に同社が配信した動画から分かるように、この技術は、サルの脳にN1リンクを埋め込み、手を使わずテレビゲームで遊ぶことを実現するまでになっている。この技術が外科手術ロボット、神経疾患の治療や、感覚・運動機能の回復にも使用される日はそう遠くではないであろう。

■ Technology / Engineering のミニ知識

映画やSFの世界で見るようなことが現実に起こったらどのような世界になるのであろうか。AIと脳と機械をつなぐBMIの技術が進歩すれば、その世界を見ることができるであろう。人間の思考や感覚を外部装置で代行すれば、ロボットアームなどを用いた機能代替、高次脳機能障害、難聴、失明、麻痺、脳卒中などの感覚・運動機能の回復、また精神・神経疾患の治療に役立ち、さらには、人間の思考を持ったロボットも実現させるであろう。この実現には、AIやBMIの技術のみならず、医用工学といった、医学と機械、電気電子、情報といった工学の分野の知識を駆使した技術が必要となる。

Words & Phrases（BMIに関する研究開発や産業などに関連した言葉）

☐ medical engineering	☐ 医用工学
☐ artificial intelligence（AI）	☐ 人工知能
☐ brain-machine interface（BMI）	☐ ブレイン・マシン・インターフェース：brain–computer interface（BCI）ともいう
☐ brain science	☐ 脳科学
☐ neuron	☐ 神経細胞
☐ neurological disorder	☐ 精神疾患
☐ synapse	☐ シナプス
☐ numbness	☐ 麻痺
☐ Parkinson disease	☐ パーキンソン病

■ Let's Think!

医用工学に関わる身近な技術や研究開発を調べて、英語で（難しければ日本語で）まとめてみよう。

Unit 4: 巨人の両手が支える橋がベトナムの新名所に

Technology / Engineering/ Arts

Listen and check the words ❶

Listen two times to the news read at natural speed. Check the box for each of the keywords below when you hear them, and look at the definition of each word to understand the news.

		definition
☐ innovative	[ˈɪnəveɪtɪv]	: introducing or using new ideas, ways of doing something, etc.
☐ horde	[hɔːd]	: a large crowd of people
☐ colossal	[kəˈlɒsl]	: extremely large
☐ evoke	[ɪˈvəʊk]	: to bring a feeling, a memory or an image into mind
☐ strip	[strɪp]	: a long narrow piece of paper, metal, cloth, etc.

Listen and check the words ❷

Listen two times to the same news read at slow speed without pauses. Check the box for each of the words and phrases below when you hear them, and write down any other information or expressions you hear.

	Notes
☐ with the help of	
☐ hordes of	
☐ above sea level	
☐ it's meant to	
☐ pulling a strip of	

Check your comprehension

What is the news about?

Headline

Choose the best headline for this news.

(A) The Mountains of Central Vietnam

(B) Unique Bridge in Vietnam

(C) Post Cards of the Mountain Pictures

(D) The Giant Golden Hands

Unit 4

Check the transcript and make sure you understand the content. Then listen to the news again and again until you can catch all of it.

Unique Bridge in Vietnam

With the help of some innovative engineering, tourists can take a walk in the clouds through the mountains of central Vietnam. This sky-high bridge in Da Nang has attracted hordes of visitors after [since] pictures were posted online. Set more than 1,400 meters above sea level, the golden walkway sits on that, a colossal pair of hands. One of the designers says it's meant to evoke giant hands of a god pulling a strip of gold out of the earth.

Aired on August 2, 2018

TOEIC-style Questions

1. Why have a lot of tourists been attracted by the bridge?

(A) Because they can buy the pictures in the mountains.

(B) Because they can enjoy walking there as if they were walking in the clouds.

(C) Because they can be innovative engineers.

(D) Because one of the designers has giants hands.

2. What is a major element of the bridge's design?

(A) Hands

(B) The sea

(C) Mountains

(D) Clouds

Transcript divided by slashes

ゆっくり音声[ポーズ入り] 12

Use this page to practice slash listening and shadowing. Circle the subject and underline the verb to understand subject-verb agreement.

巨人の両手が支える橋が ベトナムの新名所に

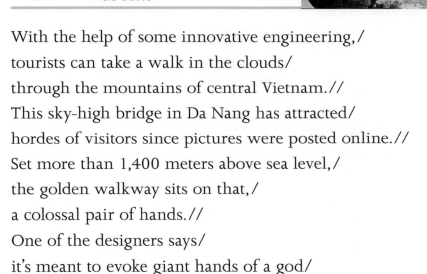

With the help of some innovative engineering,/
tourists can take a walk in the clouds/
through the mountains of central Vietnam.//
This sky-high bridge in Da Nang has attracted/
hordes of visitors since pictures were posted online.//
Set more than 1,400 meters above sea level,/
the golden walkway sits on that,/
a colossal pair of hands.//
One of the designers says/
it's meant to evoke giant hands of a god/
pulling a strip of gold out of the earth.//

語注

with the help of: ～のおかげもあって、～を利用して	**Da Nang:** ダナン ▶ベトナムの都市。	**(be)set:** (場所に) 位置している	**evoke:** (考えやイメージなどを) 想起させる
innovative: 革新的な、斬新な	**hordes of:** 非常に多くの	**above sea level:** 海抜…、標高…	**pull A out of B:** AをBから引っ張り出す
take a walk: 散歩する	**post...online:** …をインターネット上に投稿する	**colossal:** 巨大な、壮大な	**strip:** 細長い切れ、細長い一片
sky-high: とてつもなく高い		**be meant to do:** ～するように作られている	

■ ナチュラル音声のアクセント

オーストラリア英語

■ ニュースのミニ知識

ダナンのバーナーヒルズにあり2018年4月に完成した150メートルの長さの金の橋は、アバター庭園へ行くケーブルカー駅へと繋がる通路として作られた。金塊を想起させるこの橋のコンセプトは、神話の神々、人間、そして自然に着目したテーマを表し、人間を越える存在である神々は、超自然的な巨人のような存在として表されていることから、巨大な二本の手が、橋を自然からの贈りものとして崇拝するかのようにつり上げている。橋は、人工物が自然と調和するように設計された。そのため、橋脚の数を減らしながら、崖が崩壊しないように建設された。2本の腕は、コンクリート製ではなく、針金と、繊維ガラスで巻かれ、解剖学的構造に従って骨組枠で支えられ、装飾されている。さらに、指の位置は現在の位置に整うまで何度も変えられた。

■ Technology / Engineering / Arts のミニ知識

自然破壊を最小限に留め、自然と調和する景観を重視しながら、神話や宗教を想起させる芸術性と橋梁工学ならびに材料工学の技術を合わせて建設された黄金の橋は観光名所となるばかりか、自然、芸術、技術の融合した土木構造物ともなっている。身近にある道路や橋、さらには公園などの社会基盤を造り上げるのは土木工学の分野の知識が必要とされるが、ユニークな形をした構造物は、人を魅了する芸術性が付与されるほど様々な技術を必要とする。

Words & Phrases（建造物や観光に関する研究開発や産業などに関連した言葉）

□ bridge engineering	□ 橋梁工学
□ landscape engineering	□ 景観工学
□ materials science and engineering	□ 材料工学
□ fiberglass	□ 繊維ガラス
□ structure	□ 構造
□ nature conservation	□ 自然保護
□ tourist attraction	□ 観光名所
□ cable car	□ ケーブルカー
□ gods	□ 神話の神々
□ religion	□ 宗教

■ Let's Think!

自然と調和する芸術性のある建築物や構造物に関わる身近な技術や研究開発を調べて、英語で（難しければ日本語で）まとめてみよう。

Technology / Engineering / Arts

🔊 Listen and check the words ❶

ナチュラル音声

Listen two times to the news read at natural speed. Check the box for each of the keywords below when you hear them, and look at the definition of each word to understand the news.

		definition
☐ augment	[ɔːgˈment]	: to increase the amount, value, size, etc. of something
☐ place	[pleɪs]	: to put something in a particular place, especially when you do it carefully or deliberately
☐ creature	[ˈkriːtʃər]	: a living thing, real or imaginary, that can move around, such as an animal
☐ capture	[ˈkæptʃər]	: to catch a person or an animal and keep them as a prisoner or shut them in a space that they cannot escape from
☐ feature	[ˈfiːtʃər]	: to include a particular person or thing as a special feature

🔊 Listen and check the words ❷

ゆっくり音声[ポーズなし]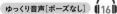

Listen two times to the same news read at slow speed without pauses. Check the box for each of the words and phrases below when you hear them, and write down any other information or expressions you hear.

☐ you've always wanted to
☐ lets you catch them
☐ all you have to do is walk
☐ do watch
☐ all players had to do was stand

Notes

Check your comprehension

What is the news about?

Headline

Choose the best headline for this news.

(A) How to Be a Pokémon Trainer

(B) Smartphone Users in Australia

(C) Hunting Creatures in a Police Station

(D) On the Hunt with Pokémon Go

Unit 5

Check the transcript and make sure you understand the content. Then listen to the news again and again until you can catch all of it.

On the Hunt with *Pokémon Go*

Now, if you've always wanted to be a Pokémon trainer, this new smartphone game lets you catch them all in real life. *Pokémon Go* uses augmented reality to place creatures in real locations, so all you have to do is walk around town and capture them. But do watch where you're going, please. After a game featured a police station in Australia as a PokéStop, police asked players to stop hunting actually inside the police station itself. All players had to do was stand outside the building to get their items.

Aired on July 7, 2016

TOEIC-style Questions

1. How do the Pokémon creatures make inroads into real life?

   (A) By walking with Pokémon trainers

   (B) By appearing through augmented reality

   (C) By watching where you're going

   (D) By asking police officers to help

2. What were Pokémon players in Australia asked NOT to do?

   (A) To walk around town hunting creatures

   (B) To place creatures in real locations

   (C) To catch creatures inside a police building

   (D) To stand outside a police station getting items

Use this page to practice slash listening and shadowing. Circle the subject and underline the verb to understand subject-verb agreement.

ポケモンGOが
現実社会を変える？

EM ALL WITH MOBILE GAME "POKEMON GO

Now, if you've always wanted to be a Pokémon trainer,/

this new smartphone game lets you catch them all in real life.//

Pokémon Go uses augmented reality/

to place creatures in real locations,/

so all you have to do/

is walk around town and capture them.//

But do watch where you're going, please.//

After a game featured a police station in Australia as a PokéStop,/

police asked players/

to stop hunting actually inside the police station itself.//

All players had to do/

was stand outside the building to get their items.//

語注

smartphone: スマートフォン	**place A in B:** AをBの中に置く、入れる	**capture:** 〜を捕らえる、捕獲する	**police station:** 警察署
augmented reality: 拡張現実、拡張現実感　▶現実世界の物事に対してコンピューターによる情報を付加すること。略称AR。	**creature:** （恐ろしい）生き物	**feature A as B:** AにBの役を演じさせる、Bという役目を与える	**item:** 品物、品目　▶ポケモンGOでは、ポケモン捕獲やポケモンを進化させたりするのに利用できる品を「アイテム」もしくは「道具」と呼ぶ。
	location: 場所、位置	**actually:** 実際に、本当に	
	walk around: 〜を歩き回る、散歩する		

■ ナチュラル音声のアクセント

オーストラリア英語

■ ニュースのミニ知識

ポケモン GO は、2015 年に株式会社ポケモン、グーグル、任天堂から 3500 万ドルを調達したナイアンティック社により開発された。2016 年 7 月 6 日のオーストラリア、ニュージーランド、米国を皮切りに、世界各地でポケモン GO のサービスが開始されると、社会現象といえるブームを巻き起こした。ポケモン GO は GPS 型 AR 技術を使い、位置情報を活用し、スマホカメラを使い、現実世界そのものを舞台としてプレイするゲームのため、歩きスマホによる事故や不法侵入事件なども多発した。2017 年にはさらに AR ＋の技術が取り入れられ、距離の概念が追加されポケモンのそばに近寄れるようになり、さらにリアルな捕獲体験ができるようになった。

■ Technology / Engineering / Arts のミニ知識

現実世界からの情報にコンピュータで情報を補足し、仮想現実に重ねて表示する AR 技術は、様々なところで利用されている。ゲームはもちろんのこと、商品販売、自動車や電子機器のマニュアル、家具や機器の設置シミュレーションなどにも利用される。この様に、素晴らしい最先端技術の応用方法も検討されなければならない。例えば、AR 技術のポケモン GO への応用は、ポケモンの人気とスマートフォンの普及がその成功の要因の一つであったといえよう。最先端の技術をどのようにして「ものづくり」に応用するか、アイディアや発想力も必要であろう。また、事故を発生させたり、日々の暮らしを脅かさないよう、公衆の安全と安心を最優先して「ものづくり」をする技術者倫理も必要となる。

Words & Phrases（AR に関する研究開発や産業などに関連した言葉）

□ human interface	□ ヒューマンインタフェース
□ virtual reality	□ 仮想現実
□ metaverse	□ メタバース
□ business intelligence（BI）	□ ビジネスインテリジェンス
□ Interactive media	□ インタラクティブメディア
□ mobile marketing	□ モバイルマーケティング
□ virtual information	□ 仮想情報
□ wearable device	□ ウェアラブル端末
□ engineering ethics	□ 技術者倫理

■ Let's Think!

スマホゲームに関わる身近な技術や研究開発を調べて、英語で（難しければ日本語で）まとめてみよう。

Listen and check the words ❶   ナチュラル音声

Listen two times to the news read at natural speed. Check the box for each of the keywords below when you hear them, and look at the definition of each word to understand the news.

		definition
☐ beetle	[ˈbiːtl]	: an insect, often large and black, with a hard case on its back, covering its wings
☐ tough	[tʌf]	: not easily cut, broken, torn, etc.
☐ credit	[ˈkredɪt]	: to believe or say that somebody is responsible for doing something, especially something good
☐ interlock	[ˌɪntəˈlɒk]	: to fit or be fastened together securely
☐ lid	[lɪd]	: a cover over a container that can be removed or opened by turning it or lifting it

 Listen and check the words ❷   ゆっくり音声［ポーズなし］

Listen two times to the same news read at slow speed without pauses. Check the box for each of the words and phrases below when you hear them, and write down any other information or expressions you hear.

☐ seems like something
☐ wanted to find out
☐ are hopeful that
☐ allow them to invent
☐ in the things we build

Notes

💡 Check your comprehension

What is the news about?

Headline

Choose the best headline for this news.

(A) Beetle Seems to Be Devil

(B) Beetle Gives Hints on Toughness

(C) Scientists Published Nature

(D) Pretty Beatle's Back

Check the transcript and make sure you understand the content. Then listen to the news again and again until you can catch all of it.

Beetle Gives Hints on Toughness

Probably seems like something called a diabolical ironclad beetle would be pretty tough. Well, it is—so tough you can run over it with a car and the beetle is still ticking. Scientists wanted to find out why, and in a new study published in the journal *Nature*, they credit two interlocking "lids" over the beetle's back for protecting it. Researchers are hopeful that studying this beetle will allow them to invent new and stronger materials for better engineering in the things we build.

Aired on October 23, 2020

TOEIC-style Questions

1. What is remarkable about this beetle?
- (A) Its back has iron lids.
- (B) It makes a ticking sound.
- (C) It can survive despite being run over.
- (D) It can open its lids.

2. Why are researchers studying this beetle?
- (A) To learn how to eradicate it
- (B) To learn how to make stronger building materials
- (C) To get hints on how to design better lids
- (D) To get hints on how to make tougher cars

Use this page to practice slash listening and shadowing. Circle the subject and underline the verb to understand subject-verb agreement.

車にひかれても平気！
頑丈すぎる甲虫の謎に挑む

Probably seems like something called a diabolical ironclad beetle would be pretty tough.//

Well, it is—/

so tough you can run over it with a car and the beetle is still ticking.//

Scientists wanted to find out why,/

and in a new study published in the journal *Nature*,/

they credit two interlocking "lids" over the beetle's back for protecting it.//

Researchers are hopeful/

that studying this beetle will allow them to invent new and stronger materials/

for better engineering in the things we build.//

Unit 6

語注

toughness:《タイトル》強じん性、硬さ	**pretty:** かなり、相当	**credit...for doing:** 〜できるのは…のおかげだと見なす	**allow...to do:** …が〜できるようにする
diabolical ironclad beetle: コブゴミムシダマシ ▶英名の意味は「悪魔のような装甲の甲虫（こうちゅう）」。	**run over:**（車などで）〜をひく **tick:**（カチカチいう時計のように）きちんと作動する、正常に動く	**interlocking:** かみ合っている、連結している **lid:** ふた、ふた状のもの	**be hopeful that:** 〜ということを期待している **material:** 素材、材料

■ ナチュラル音声のアクセント

アメリカ英語

■ ニュースのミニ知識

2020年10月、東京農工大学と米国カリフォルニア大学アーバイン校などの国際共同研究チームが、極めて頑丈な外骨格を持つ甲虫（こうちゅう）の一種（学名 *Phloeodes diabolicus*）を研究し、その頑丈さをもたらす仕組みを解明したと発表した。別名「Ironclad beetle（鋼鉄で武装した甲虫）」と呼ばれるこの甲虫は、捕食者から身を守るため、進化するうちに頑強な外骨格を獲得したと考えられる。その外骨格の強固性の要因は、接合部の構造、内部のミクロな層状構造、構成物質によるものであり、その仕組みの応用により、自動車や航空機などの製造に用いる高強度・軽量材料の開発が望める。また、外骨格接合部の構造を模倣した材料により、部材を強固に接合できることも実証された。

■ Science / Technology / Engineering のミニ知識

生存するために進化した生物の構造や機能、生産プロセスを学び、新しい技術の開発と物づくりに生かすバイオミメティックス（生物模倣）技術の分野が注目されている。バイオミメティックスは、1950年代後半に提唱されたが、翼や羽といった生物の外見の模倣から始まり、電子顕微鏡の発明以降は細胞機能にまで研究が及んでいる。例えば、ハスの葉を模倣した超撥水表面をヨーグルトのフタに利用したり、アホウドリの翼の形状をエアコン室外機のプロペラファンに適用したりと生物の構造や機能が製品の開発に活かされている。そのほか、ドローンにハチドリのホバリング機能、痛みの少ない注射針開発に蚊の吸血針の機能を模倣して活用されている。このようにバイオミメティックスは、工学や医療分野などに幅広く応用されている。

Words & Phrases（バイオミメティックスに関する研究開発や産業などに関連した言葉）

☐ biomimetics	☐ バイオミメティックス（生物模倣）
☐ biomechanics	☐ 生体力学
☐ biophysics	☐ 生物物理学
☐ biodiversity	☐ 生物多様性
☐ natural selection	☐ 自然淘汰
☐ biological tissue	☐ 生体組織
☐ cell function	☐ 細胞機能
☐ artificial photosynthesis	☐ 人工光合成
☐ electron microscope	☐ 電子顕微鏡

■ Let's Think!

生物模倣に関わる身近な技術や研究開発を調べて、英語で（難しければ日本語で）まとめてみよう。

Unit 7: 日本企業による「空飛ぶ車」の実用化が間近!?

Technology / Engineering / Arts

🔊 Listen and check the words ❶

ナチュラル音声

Listen two times to the news read at natural speed. Check the box for each of the keywords below when you hear them, and look at the definition of each word to understand the news.

		definition
☐ staple	['steɪpl]	: a large or important part of something
☐ accessible	[ək'sesəbl]	: that can be reached, entered, used, seen, etc.
☐ means	[miːnz]	: an action, an object or a system by which a result is achieved
☐ transportation	[ˌtrænspɔːˈteɪʃn]	: a system for carrying people or goods from one place to another using vehicles, roads, etc.
☐ launch	[lɔːntʃ]	: to make a product or service available to the public for the first time

🔊 Listen and check the words ❷

ゆっくり音声[ポーズなし]

Listen two times to the same news read at slow speed without pauses. Check the box for each of the words and phrases below when you hear them, and write down any other information or expressions you hear.

	Notes
☐ have been a staple	
☐ one step closer to	
☐ making this fantasy a reality	
☐ to help create a society	
☐ with the hopes of	

💡 Check your comprehension

What is the news about?	Headline
	Choose the best headline for this news.
	(A) Important Character of Science Fiction
	(B) A Test Pilot of Flying Car
	(C) Successful Test of Flying Car
	(D) Introduction of a Successful CEO

Check the transcript and make sure you understand the content. Then listen to the news again and again until you can catch all of it.

Successful Test of Flying Car

Well, flying cars have been a staple in science fiction for years. Now, a Japanese company is one step closer to making this fantasy a reality. Watch as the pilot of this car takes it out for a test flight. The CEO of the company says his goal is to help create a society where flying cars are a safe and accessible means of transportation. The company will continue to develop the car, with the hopes of launching in 2023.

Aired on August 31, 2020

TOEIC-style Questions

1. What is reported about this flying car?

(A) It will be used in a science-fiction movie.

(B) It is in the early stages of development.

(C) It has already been flown in a test flight.

(D) It is a safe means of transportation.

2. When does the company hope to start selling this flying car?

(A) It has already started selling it.

(B) In 2023.

(C) The information is not provided.

(D) The company does not intend to sell it.

Use this page to practice slash listening and shadowing. Circle the subject and underline the verb to understand subject-verb agreement.

日本企業による「空飛ぶ車」の実用化が間近!?

Well, flying cars have been a staple in science fiction/
for years.//
Now, a Japanese company is one step closer/
to making this fantasy a reality.//
Watch as the pilot of this car takes it out for a test flight.//
The CEO of the company says/
his goal is to help create a society/
where flying cars are a safe and accessible means of
transportation.//
The company will continue to develop the car,/
with the hopes of launching in 2023.//

Unit 7

語注

successful:《タイトル》成功した、うまくいった	**science fiction:** 空想科学小説、SF	**take...out:** …を外へ出す	**transportation:** 輸送、交通
flying car:《タイトル》空飛ぶクルマ	**be one step closer to:** 〜に一歩近づいている	**test flight:** 試験飛行	**with the hopes of:** 〜を期待して、〜を目標にして
staple: なくてはならない要素、定番のもの	**fantasy:** 夢想、空想	**accessible:** 利用しやすい、入手しやすい	**launch:** 〜を売り出す、発売する
	reality: 現実、現実のこと	**means:** 方法、手段	

■ ナチュラル音声のアクセント

オーストラリア英語

■ ニュースのミニ知識

映画やアニメで登場する「空飛ぶクルマ」が現実のものになりつつあり、ウーバー社など世界各国で開発が進められている。日本では、官民協議会や政府閣議決定の未来投資戦略で、「空飛ぶクルマ」の実現に動きだし、2023年から事業開始と、2030年代には実用化を拡大させることを目指している。この「空飛ぶクルマ」の実現に向け、2020年8月、スタートアップ企業のSkyDrive社がトヨタなどに先がけて有人飛行の公開試験を成功させた。電動のため低騒音・低コスト、運転が簡単、垂直離発着が可能などの利点を持つ空飛ぶ車だが、SkyDrive社によれば、2021年10月、国土交通省航空局に2人乗りの「SkyDrive式SD-05型機」の型式証明申請が受理され、さらに、2022年3月には、「耐空性審査要領第II部」ベースでの構築が合意に至り、2025年の事業開始を目指している。

■ Technology / Engineering / Arts のミニ知識

「空飛ぶクルマ」は、電動・垂直離着陸型・無操縦者航空機などによる都市型航空交通、観光、物流への活用が期待される。実際、ドローンで、山間部への建設資材運搬や災害地へ物資運搬などに活用されるように無人航空機は身近なものになってきている。eVTOLには、電気自動車をベースにして、バッテリーを搭載し、プロペラと自動制御システムを備えた機種がある。「空飛ぶクルマ」実現の課題として、機体の軽量化やバッテリーなどの技術の向上、また、離発着場や航空管制システム、充電設備といったインフラ整備、さらに法整備やルール整備、また安全性の確保なども必要となる。航空産業のみならず、自動車産業、観光産業、町づくりといった裾野が広い事業のなかで、官民で取り組み、安全に利用できる「空飛ぶクルマ」実現に向けて、様々な開発が求められている。

Words & Phrases （eVTOLに関する研究開発や産業などに関連した言葉）

□ electric vertical takeoff and landing (eVTOL) □ 電動垂直離着陸

□ electric vehicle (EV) □ 電気自動車

□ unmanned aerial vehicles (UAV) □ 無人飛行機

□ urban air mobility (UAM) □ アーバン・エア・モビリティ：人や物を空を使って輸送する都市交通システム

□ air taxi □ エアタクシー

□ traffic control □ 交通制御

□ automobile industry □ 自動車産業

□ aviation safety □ 航空安全

■ Let's Think!

ドローンに関わる身近な技術や研究開発を調べて、英語で（難しければ日本語で）まとめてみよう。

🔊 Listen and check the words ❶

ナチュラル音声 23

Listen two times to the news read at natural speed. Check the box for each of the keywords below when you hear them, and look at the definition of each word to understand the news.

		definition
☐ limb	[lɪm]	: an arm or a leg
☐ virtual	[ˈvɜːtʃuəl]	: made to appear to exist by the use of computer software
☐ simulator	[ˈsɪmjuleɪtər]	: a piece of equipment that artificially creates a particular set of conditions in order to train somebody to deal with a situation that they may experience in reality
☐ exoskeleton	[ˈeksəʊskelɪtn]	: a machine attached to somebody's body to enable them to perform movements and actions more easily
☐ translate	[trænzˈleɪt]	: to change something into a different form

🔊 Listen and check the words ❷

ゆっくり音声［ポーズなし］ 25

Listen two times to the same news read at slow speed without pauses. Check the box for each of the words and phrases below when you hear them, and write down any other information or expressions you hear.

	Notes
☐ the use of	
☐ he's been able to	
☐ he's been working with	
☐ reach for	
☐ translates brain signals into	

Unit 8

Check your comprehension

What is the news about?	Headline
	Choose the best headline for this news.
	(A) A Man Lost His Limbs Again
	(B) Working with Virtual Simulators for Four Years
	(C) Quadriplegic Uses Brain Tech to Walk
	(D) An Implanted Recording Device in His Limbs

Check the transcript and make sure you understand the content. Then listen to the news again and again until you can catch all of it.

Quadriplegic Uses Brain Tech to Walk

A man who lost the use of all four limbs in a fall four years ago—well, he's been able to walk and move his limbs again. He's known only as Thibault. He's been working with virtual simulators and an exoskeleton for two years. He's now walked 145 meters, and he can reach for targets with his arms. Researchers did this: they implanted a recording device in his head that translates brain signals into movements of the suit.

Aired on October 5, 2019

TOEIC-style Questions

1. When did Thibault lose his ability to walk?
   (A) When he was a child
   (B) Two years ago
   (C) Four years ago
   (D) Five years ago

2. What has made it possible for Thibault to walk again?
   (A) Simulators
   (B) An exoskeleton
   (C) A recording device
   (D) All of the above

Use this page to practice slash listening and shadowing. Circle the subject and underline the verb to understand subject-verb agreement.

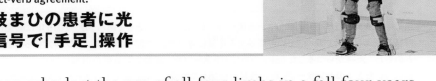

四肢まひの患者に光
脳信号で「手足」操作

A man who lost the use of all four limbs in a fall four years ago/

—well, he's been able to walk and move his limbs again.//

He's known only as Thibault.//

He's been working with virtual simulators/

and an exoskeleton for two years.//

He's now walked 145 meters,/

and he can reach for targets with his arms.//

Researchers did this:/

they implanted a recording device in his head/

that translates brain signals into movements of the suit.//

Unit
8

語注

quadriplegic:《タイトル》四肢まひの人	**fall:** 転落	**target:** 目標物、対象	**brain signal:** 脳信号
use: ①〜を用いる　②(手足・器官などの) 使用能力	**virtual simulator:** 仮想シミュレーター	**implant A in B:** AをBに埋め込む	**movement:** 動作
limb: 肢(し)、手足	**exoskeleton:** (人工) 外骨格、パワードスーツ	**recording device:** 記録装置	**suit:** スーツ　▶ここでは exoskeletonのこと。
	reach for: 〜に手を伸ばす	**translate A into B:** AをBに変換する、転換する	

■ ナチュラル音声のアクセント

オーストラリア英語

■ ニュースのミニ知識

頭の中で考えるだけで、麻痺している体が動くようになったらどうであろうか。2015年に転落により、脊髄を損傷したティボーはその可能性を4年後に見せた。フランスのグルノーブル大学らの研究チームのもと、天井からつるした65kgのパワードスーツを、運動を司る脳の領域に埋め込んだ64の電極のついた2つのセンサーで、脳の信号を収集して解読し、480歩で145メートル歩いてみせたのだ。もちろん、ここに至るまで2年かかり、その間、コンピューターゲームでアバターをセンサーで制御し、39回もの実験を行った。それでも、ティボーは「月面を歩いた最初の人間のようだ」と喜びを声にした。一方、課題もあり、スーツのバランスを取るのが難しく、屋外での使用が実現していない。

■ Science / Technology / Engineering / Arts のミニ知識

パラリンピックで活躍する選手達は、車いすや義肢を用いてバスケットボールやテニス、陸上競技や卓球を行い、めざましい成績を見せている。AIとBMIの技術が進歩すれば、パラリンピックに出場できなかった障害を持つ人たちも活躍できるのであろうか。また、健康・生命維持のため、レントゲン、MRI、CTスキャン、人工呼吸器、人工心肺装置などの医療機器がある。後者の生命維持管理装置は臨床工学技士が扱う機器である。身近にある医療機器には、医用工学の技術と医師・看護師、そしてそれを扱う技士も時に必要となる。

Words & Phrases （医工学に関する研究開発や産業などに関連した言葉）

☐ brainwave	☐ 脳波
☐ neural system	☐ 神経システム
☐ spinal cord	☐ 脊髄
☐ artificial limb	☐ 義肢
☐ clinical trial	☐ 臨床試験
☐ medical appliance	☐ 医療機器
☐ life support equipment	☐ 生命維持装置
☐ mechanical ventilator	☐ 人工呼吸器
☐ magnetic resonance imaging（MRI）	☐ 磁気共鳴画像法
☐ clinical engineer	☐ 臨床工学士

■ Let's Think!

障害を持った人たちを支援する身近な技術や研究開発を調べて、英語で（難しければ日本語で）まとめてみよう。

Technology / Engineering

🔊 Listen and check the words ❶

ナチュラル音声 〖26〗

Listen two times to the news read at natural speed. Check the box for each of the keywords below when you hear them, and look at the definition of each word to understand the news.

definition

☐ green [griːn] : connected with the protection of the environment
☐ incline ['ɪnklaɪn] : a slope
☐ congestion [kənˈdʒestʃən] : the state of being crowded and full of traffic
☐ bunch [bʌntʃ] : a large number of things or people
☐ ecofriendly [ˌiːkəʊ ˈfrendli] : not harmful to the environment

🔊 Listen and check the words ❷

ゆっくり音声［ポーズなし］ 〖28〗

Listen two times to the same news read at slow speed without pauses. Check the box for each of the words and phrases below when you hear them, and write down any other information or expressions you hear.

	Notes
☐ going green	
☐ the same as	
☐ a whole bunch of	
☐ will first roll out	
☐ how healthy or unhealthy the air is	

Unit 9

 Check your comprehension

What is the news about?

Headline

Choose the best headline for this news.

(A) Going to Forests with Google Maps

(B) Google Maps Helps the Most Ecofriendly Cars

(C) Google Maps Gets Ecofriendly

(D) The Firstest Way to Find Air Pollution

Check the transcript and make sure you understand the content. Then listen to the news again and again until you can catch all of it.

Google Maps Gets Ecofriendly

Google Maps [is] going green, with directions defaulting to the most fuel-efficient option if travel time is the same as the fastest route. Road incline, traffic congestion [and] a whole bunch of other factors will be considered in deciding that route. The ecofriendly defaults will first roll out in the United States. Google will also launch an air-quality layer to show just how healthy or unhealthy the air is during your trip.

Aired on March 31, 2021

TOEIC-style Questions

1. What change was planned for Google Maps?
   - (A) Directions will be shown in green.
   - (B) Fuel-efficient routes will be given higher priority.
   - (C) The fastest route will no longer be the default option.
   - (D) Only routes with good air quality will be shown.

2. According to this news report, what factor will be used in deciding default routes?
   - (A) Air quality
   - (B) Time of day
   - (C) Amount of traffic
   - (D) All of the above

Use this page to practice slash listening and shadowing. Circle the subject and underline the verb to understand subject-verb agreement.

Googleマップに新機能！
エコフレンドリーなルートとは？

E CHANGE
: MAPS TO DEFAULT TO "ECO-FRIENDLY" ROU

Google Maps is going green,/

with directions defaulting to the most fuel-efficient option/

if travel time is the same as the fastest route.//

Road incline,/

traffic congestion/

and a whole bunch of other factors/

will be considered in deciding that route.//

The ecofriendly defaults will first roll out in the

United States.//

Google will also launch an air-quality layer/

to show just how healthy or unhealthy the air is/

during your trip.//

Unit
9

語注

go green: 自然や環境に配慮する ようになる **directions:** 道順(の案内) **default:** ①《default to》〜を初 期状態とする ②初期 設定、デフォルト	**fuel-efficient:** 燃費のよい、低燃費の **incline:** 傾斜(度) **traffic congestion:** 交通渋滞 **a whole bunch of:** 《話》たくさんの、いろ いろな	**ecofriendly:** 環境に優しい **roll out:** 〈新製品などが〉発売 される、(新サービスな どの)提供が始まる **launch:** 〜を開始する、公開する	**air quality:** 大気質、空気汚染度 **layer:** レイヤー ▶グラフィ ックソフトウェアなどに 搭載されている、画像 をセル画のように重ね て使うことができる機 能のこと。

■ ナチュラル音声のアクセント

オーストラリア英語

■ ニュースのミニ知識

2020年9月、グーグル社は、アメリカ国立再生可能エネルギー研究所と協力して、2022年までに10億人のグーグルユーザーに人間の活動が地球環境にかける負担を減らす方法を提供すると発表した。2021年10月に始まったグーグルマップアプリで環境に優しいルート選択をオンにすると、ルートの燃料効率が推定値で表示され、燃料消費量とCO_2排出量を低く抑えられるルートを選択できる。地上の内燃機関エンジンから排出されるCO_2は、世界のCO_2排出量の18%を占めている。同社は、2007年より脱炭素化に取り組み、2030年までにカーボンフリーエネルギー事業を各地で展開し、持続可能なカーボンフリー社会の実現のために、有限な資源の再利用に加えて水資源の確保や水の安全保障を支援している。

■ Technology / Engineering のミニ知識

気候変動に関する政府間パネル（IPCC）は、2011年から2020年の平均気温は、産業革命以前の気温と比べて1.09℃の上昇が見られると報告している。そして地球温暖化ガスの排出量を大幅に削減しないと、2030年代始めまでには気温は産業革命以前より1.5℃上昇し、気候変動が継続すると予想している。一方、多くの企業や国家がカーボンフリーを目指し、さらに、SDGs達成のために産学官や個人も取り組んできている。また、健康で持続可能な社会を目指すLOHASな活動や研究も行われている。IEAによると、交通機関から排出されるCO_2排出量は2018-19年にピークに達し、その後徐々に減っていくと予想されているが、CO_2排出量を抑えるための技術革新は急務となっている。

Words & Phrases（カーボンフリーに関する研究開発や産業などに関連した言葉）

- ☐ IEA（International Energy Agency） ☐ 国際エネルギー機関
- ☐ CO_2 emission ☐ 二酸化炭素排出
- ☐ environmental footprint ☐ 環境フットプリント
- ☐ carbon-free energy ☐ カーボンフリーエネルギー
- ☐ water security ☐ 水の安全保障
- ☐ electrification ☐ 電化
- ☐ mitigation ☐ 緩和
- ☐ adaptation ☐ 適応
- ☐ LOHAS（lifestyles of health and sustainability） ☐ 健康で持続可能性のある生活様式

■ Let's Think!

脱炭素化に関わる身近な技術や研究開発を調べて、英語で（難しければ日本語で）まとめてみよう。

Listen and check the words ❶

ナチュラル音声 29

Listen two times to the news read at natural speed. Check the box for each of the keywords below when you hear them, and look at the definition of each word to understand the news.

		definition
☐ cave	[keɪv]	: a large hole in the side of a hill or cliff or under the ground
☐ dwelling	['dwelɪŋ]	: a house, flat, etc. where a person lives
☐ reveal	[rɪ'viːl]	: to make something known to somebody
☐ modify	['mɒdɪfaɪ]	: to change something slightly, especially in order to make it more suitable for a particular purpose
☐ note	[nəʊt]	: a single sound of a particular length and pitch, made by the voice or a musical instrument

 Listen and check the words ❷

ゆっくり音声[ポーズなし] 31

Listen two times to the same news read at slow speed without pauses. Check the box for each of the words and phrases below when you hear them, and write down any other information or expressions you hear.

☐ has been played
☐ for the first time
☐ in a Stone Age cave dwelling
☐ it's been modified
☐ one of the shell's openings

Notes

Unit
10

💡 **Check your comprehension**

What is the news about?

Headline

Choose the best headline for this news.

(A) Stone Age Musical Instrument

(B) Shells in A Stone Age Cave Dwelling

(C) Musical Notes Reveled by A CT Scan

(D) How to Open Shells in France

Check the transcript and make sure you understand the content. Then listen to the news again and again until you can catch all of it.

Stone Age Musical Instrument

Scientists say a Stone Age musical instrument has been played for the first time in 18,000 years. This conch shell was discovered in 1931 in a Stone Age cave dwelling in France. A modern CT scan revealed it's been modified to produce musical notes—like this. Researchers say they found traces of resin around one of the shell's openings. They believe that was probably where a mouthpiece was once attached.

Aired on February 12, 2021

TOEIC-style Questions

1. What did the CT scan show about the conch shell?
   (A) It came from France.
   (B) It is at least 18,000 years old.
   (C) It was changed to function as a musical instrument.
   (D) It is the earliest known musical instrument.

2. What do researchers think the resin was used for?
   (A) To attach a mouthpiece
   (B) To close one of the shell's openings
   (C) To attach the shell to the wall of a cave
   (D) To modify the shell so it could produce musical notes

Use this page to practice slash listening and shadowing. Circle the subject and underline the verb to understand subject-verb agreement.

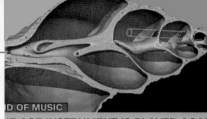

1万8000年前！
よみがえる石器時代の楽器の音色

D OF MUSIC

NE AGE INSTRUMENT IS PLAYED AGAI

Scientists say a Stone Age musical instrument/

has been played for the first time in 18,000 years.//

This conch shell was discovered in 1931/

in a Stone Age cave dwelling in France.//

A modern CT scan/

revealed it's been modified to produce musical notes—like this.//

Researchers say they found traces of resin around one of the shell's openings.//

They believe/

that was probably where a mouthpiece/

was once attached.//

語注

Stone Age:《タイトル》石器時代の	**conch shell:** ほら貝、巻き貝	**reveal (that):** ～ということを明らかにする	**note:** (楽器などの) 音、音色、楽音
musical instrument: 楽器	**cave dwelling:** 洞窟住居	**modify:** ～を改造する、修正する	**trace:** 痕跡
for the first time in...years: …年ぶりに	**CT scan:** CTスキャン ▶CTは computed tomography（コンピューター断層撮影法）の略。	**produce:** (音を) 生み出す、もたらす	**resin:** 樹脂、松やに
			opening: 開口部、穴

■ ナチュラル音声のアクセント

オーストラリア英語

■ ニュースのミニ知識

1万8,000年前のほら貝は、1931年フランスのピレネー山脈麓の先史時代の壁画が描かれているマルスラ洞穴の入り口で見つかった。発見当初考古学者達は、人間の手により加工されていないものと考え、洞穴の住人が、なんらかの儀式で使用したのではないかと推測していた。博物館に80年以上も置かれていたこのほら貝は、キャロル・フリッツ氏らのトゥールーズ大学などの研究チームによって、貝の開口部の内側に壁画に使われていた顔料の痕跡が見つかり、また貝の先端が人工的に壊されており、CTスキャンで貝の中を探ると、内部の気室に穴が開けられていたことが発見され、貝が音楽を奏でるのに使われたと結論づけられた。貝の先端の穴に筒のようなものを挿入して、吹き口にしていたと推測し、ホルン奏者に演奏を依頼すると、ド、ドのシャープ、レの音に近い3つの音がでた。

■ Science / Technology / Engineering / Arts のミニ知識

放射性炭素年代測定では、ベータ線計測法（ガスプロポーショナルカウンティング法・液体シンチレーションカウンティング法）と加速器質量分析（AMS）法を用いて、試料の放射性炭素（C14）の量を測定して、年代を推定する。放射性炭素年代測定は考古学、人類学、水文学、地質学といった幅広い分野で利用されている。また、CTスキャンは、肉眼で観察できない内部の構造を明らかにできるため、エジプトのミイラ研究や考古遺物研究などにも活用されている。また、3Dプリンターで考古遺物の復元をしたり、リモートセンシングやレーザースキャン技術を用いてピラミッドを3次元計測など、科学技術の進歩と共に、様々な知られざる太古の解明へとつながっている。

Words & Phrases（考古学に関する研究開発や産業などに関連した言葉）

☐ archaeology	☐ 考古学
☐ musicology	☐ 音楽学
☐ radiocarbon dating	☐ 放射性炭素年代測定
☐ gas proportional counting	☐ ガスプロポーショナルカウンティング法
☐ liquid scintillation counting	☐ 液体シンチレーションカウンティング法
☐ accelerator mass spectrometry	☐ 加速器質量分析（AMS）
☐ relic	☐ 遺物
☐ excavation	☐ 発掘、出土品、遺跡
☐ World Heritage	☐ 世界遺産

■ Let's Think!

文化遺産に関わる身近な技術や研究開発を調べて、英語で（難しければ日本語で）まとめてみよう。

Unit 11: ホログラム技術、コロナ禍のライブ業界を救う!?

🔊 Listen and check the words ❶

ナチュラル音声 32

Listen two times to the news read at natural speed. Check the box for each of the keywords below when you hear them, and look at the definition of each word to understand the news.

		definition
☐ while	[waɪl]	: a period of time
☐ hologram	['hɔləgræm]	: a special type of image that appears to be three-dimensional especially one created using lasers
☐ bid	[bɪd]	: an effort to do something or to obtain something
☐ coronavirus	[kə'rəʊnəvaɪrəs]	: a type of virus that can cause pneumonia and other diseases in humans and animals
☐ project	[prə'dʒekt]	: to make light, an image, etc. fall onto a flat surface or screen

🔊 Listen and check the words ❷

ゆっくり音声[ポーズなし] 34

Listen two times to the same news read at slow speed without pauses. Check the box for each of the words and phrases below when you hear them, and write down any other information or expressions you hear.

☐ it has been a while since
☐ here's one way to
☐ in the latest bid to
☐ teamed up with
☐ to put on a performance

Notes

 Check your comprehension

What is the news about?

Headline

Choose the best headline for this news.

(A) A Magic Show on the Stage

(B) Concerts Staged by Hologram

(C) A British Audience Projected by Hologram

(D) Live Concerts in the 1860s

Unit 11

Check the transcript and make sure you understand the content. Then listen to the news again and again until you can catch all of it.

Concerts Staged by Hologram

Well, if it has been a while since you've seen a live concert because of COVID-19, here's one way to see live musicians again. It's not magic; it's a hologram. In the latest bid to save concerts from the coronavirus, the company Musion 3D teamed up with singer Dan Olsen to put on a performance projected live before a British audience. And while the technology is new, it uses stage-illusion techniques that date back, yes, to the 1860s.

Aired on October 30, 2020

TOEIC-style Questions

1. What kind of performance is this news report about?
   (A) A play from the 1860s
   (B) A music concert
   (C) A magic show
   (D) A presentation about new technology

2. What kind of technology was used in this performance?
   (A) Hologram technology
   (B) Stage-illusion technology
   (C) Projection technology
   (D) All of the above

Use this page to practice slash listening and shadowing. Circle the subject and underline the verb to understand subject-verb agreement.

ホログラム技術、
コロナ禍のライブ業界を救う！？

Well, if it has been a while since you've seen a live concert because of COVID-19, /

here's one way to see live musicians again. //

It's not magic; /

it's a hologram. //

In the latest bid to save concerts from the coronavirus, /

the company Musion 3D teamed up with singer Dan Olsen /

to put on a performance projected live before a British audience. //

And while the technology is new, /

it uses stage-illusion techniques that date back, yes, to the 1860s. //

Unit 11

語注

stage:《タイトル》〜を開催する、上演する	**live:**①生の、実演の、ライブの ②生で、実演で	**in a bid to do:**〜することを目指して	**project:**〜を投映する、映写する
hologram:ホログラム	**COVID-19:**＝coronavirus disease 2019 新型コロナウイルス感染症	**save A from B:**AをBから救う	**stage-illusion:**舞台イリュージョンの、ステージマジックの
It has been a while since:〜以来ずいぶん日がたつ		**team up with:**〜と協力する、手を組む	**technique:**技術、技巧
		put on:〜を上演する、披露する	**date back to:**〜にさかのぼる

■ ナチュラル音声のアクセント

オーストラリア英語

■ ニュースのミニ知識

2014年、マイケル・ジャクソンのホログラムでの復活ステージは大きな話題となった。英国MUSION 3D社は、ステージ上の空間に立体映像を出現させる3Dホログラムの技術を世界中に展開している業界最大手企業である。エルビス・プレスリーやホイットニー・ヒューストンといった亡くなったアーティストのホログラム上演があったなか、ダン・オルセンとギタリストは、ロンドン東部のスタジオでライブ演奏すると同時に、ピアノ奏者のいる数キロ離れたロンドンの中心地のステージにホログラムで出現した。コロナ渦でステージ上演が困難な時期に、このホログラム上演は、カーボンニュートラルのツアーで、世界中どこででも可能な新たなライブの上演形態の試みとなった。

■ Technology / Engineering / Arts のミニ知識

3Dホログラムは、VR、AR、MRとは異なる最新技術である。1947年に物理学者ガボール・デーネシュによって発明されたホログラフィーは、今や3Dホログラム上演にまで進歩している。舞台上映では、ペッパーズ・ゴーストのような視覚トリックを使ったディズニーランドにあるような古くからある舞台装置を応用して、光の振幅や光の波長データに光の位相データを加え、記録・再生して3Dホログラム上演を実現させている。一方、まだ画像が鮮明ではなく、さらなる技術の進歩が望まれる。近年ホログラムで外見だけは若いデジタルアバターを利用したABBA復活ツアーが行なわれるなどしており、今後、ミュージカルやコンサート、さらにはシェイクスピア劇などの演劇にも、ホログラムや最新技術を使用した上演がますます増え、あらたな舞台装置や芸術表現様式が出現してくるであろう。

Words & Phrases（ホログラムに関する研究開発や産業などに関連した言葉）

□ holography　　　　　　　　　　　□ ホログラフィー（光の立体記録技術）

□ optics　　　　　　　　　　　　　□ 光学

□ Mixed Reality (MR)　　　　　　　□ 複合現実

□ Substitutional Reality (SR)　　　　□ 代替現実

□ three dimensional image　　　　　□ 3D 映像

□ wavefront　　　　　　　　　　　□ 波面

□ interference pattern　　　　　　　□ 干渉波

□ amplitude　　　　　　　　　　　□ 振幅

□ stage setting　　　　　　　　　　□ 舞台装置

■ Let's Think!

ホログラムに関わる身近な技術や研究開発を調べて、英語で（難しければ日本語で）まとめてみよう。

Unit 12: 自撮り画像のコーヒーアートでインスタ映え

Technology / Engineering / Arts

🔊 Listen and check the words ❶

ナチュラル音声

Listen two times to the news read at natural speed. Check the box for each of the keywords below when you hear them, and look at the definition of each word to understand the news.

		definition
☐ selfie	['selfi]	: a photo of yourself that you take, typically with a smartphone or webcam
☐ blend	[blend]	: a mixture of different types of the same thing
☐ upload	[ˌʌp'ləʊd]	: to send data to another computer
☐ foam	[fəʊm]	: a mass of very small air bubbles on the surface of a liquid
☐ mind	[maɪnd]	: to be upset, annoyed or worried by something

🔊 Listen and check the words ❷

ゆっくり音声［ポーズなし］ 37

Listen two times to the same news read at slow speed without pauses. Check the box for each of the words and phrases below when you hear them, and write down any other information or expressions you hear.

	Notes
☐ could be your perfect "blend"	
☐ the first in Europe	
☐ are uploaded to	
☐ on top of	
☐ don't seem to	

💡 Check your comprehension

What is the news about?

Headline

Choose the best headline for this news.

(A) Best Places for Afternoon Tea in London

(B) A Selfie in Your Coffee

(C) Coffee Lovers in London

(D) Taking Photos in London Coffee Shop

Check the transcript and make sure you understand the content. Then listen to the news again and again until you can catch all of it.

A Selfie in Your Coffee

If you love taking selfies and you love drinking cappuccinos, then this London coffee shop could be your perfect "blend." The teahouse is the first in Europe to offer the "selfieccino." Customers take selfies that are uploaded to a machine, and then their image is scanned and recreated on top of the foam in the drink. And people don't seem to mind the four-minute wait. The café says customers have ordered more than 400 selfieccinos since Saturday. What a great idea.

Aired on December 20, 2017

TOEIC-style Questions

1. Where is this coffee shop?
   (A) In Italy
   (B) In the United States
   (C) In London
   (D) The information is not provided.

2. What special service does this coffee shop offer?
   (A) Uploading photos of customers enjoying coffee
   (B) Making tea with foam
   (C) Letting customers make their own coffee blends
   (D) Creating images of customers in their drinks

Transcript divided by slashes ゆっくり音声[ポーズ入り] 36

Use this page to practice slash listening and shadowing. Circle the subject and underline the verb to understand subject-verb agreement.

自撮り画像のコーヒーアートで インスタ映え

If you love taking selfies and you love drinking cappuccinos, /
then this London coffee shop could be your perfect "blend."//
The teahouse is the first in Europe/
to offer the "selfieccino."//
Customers take selfies that are uploaded to a machine, /
and then their image is scanned/
and recreated on top of the foam in the drink.//
And people don't seem to mind the four-minute wait.//
The café says/
customers have ordered more than 400 selfieccinos since Saturday.//
What a great idea.//

語注

selfie:《タイトル》自撮り画像、セルフィー	**selfieccino:** ▶ selfie と cappuccino を組み合わせた造語。	**image:** 画像	**foam:** 泡
cappuccino: カプチーノ	**customer:** 客、顧客	**scan:** ～をスキャンする	**mind:** ～を嫌がる、気にする
blend: 混ぜたもの、ブレンド	**upload A to B:** AをBにアップロードする、AのデータをBに転送する	**recreate:** ～を再現する、再生する	**wait:** 待つこと、待ち時間
teahouse: 茶室、喫茶店		**on top of:** ～の上に、上部に	**café:** カフェ、喫茶店

■ ナチュラル音声のアクセント

アメリカ英語

■ ニュースのミニ知識

ロンドンにはカフェがいたる所にある。その中で、セルフィチーノを開始したのはオックスフォードストリートにあるカフェ「ティーテラス」だ。スマートフォンで客が送信した画像データをコーヒーマシンに転送・スキャンし、ハイテクフードプリンターで無味の食物用色素を使って顔が描かれる仕組みだという。飲み物はカプチーノかホットココアを選ぶことができる。オーナーのショウリーさんは、「いまや良質の食事とサービスを提供するだけでは十分ではない。インスタ映えしなければならないのだ（It's got to be Instagram-worthy）」と述べている。「ティーテラス」は5店舗あり、その中の1つの店舗ではロボットウェイトレスがセルフィチーノを運んでくれるようだ。

■ Technology / Engineering / Arts のミニ知識

レインボーラテや3Dラテといったラテアートを楽しみにカフェを訪れる人もいるでしょう。アートを手で作る職人の技もあれば、3Dラテアートマシーンで作る技術もある。スマートフォンでアプリをダウンロードしてわずか15秒でラテアートが完成する。最近では、QRコードのスキャンのみでもマシーンの使用ができる。3Dフードプリンターは、ケーキやマカロンといったものにもプリントする。インクは天然由来成分のものを使うので安心そうである。3Dプリンターの技術と、大豆などを利用したフードインクといった農学や食品科学の分野の研究が、食品のアートをより豊かにしている。また、フードとテクノロジーを融合させた代替肉製造でも注目されているフードテックの技術も注目されている。

Words & Phrases（食品に関する研究開発や産業などに関連した言葉）

□ food science	□ 食品科学
□ Food Science and Technology	□ 食品科学工学
□ FoodTech	□ フードテック
□ food microbiology	□ 食品微生物学
□ edible ink	□ 食用インク
□ food processing	□ 食品加工
□ food additive	□ 食品添加物
□ meat substitute	□ 代替肉
□ additive manufacturing	□ 付加製造
□ product development	□ 商品展開

■ Let's Think!

食品に関わる身近な技術や研究開発を調べて、英語で（難しければ日本語で）まとめてみよう。

🔊 Listen and check the words ❶

ナチュラル音声 38

Listen two times to the news read at natural speed. Check the box for each of the keywords below when you hear them, and look at the definition of each word to understand the news.

		definition
☐ former	['fɔːrmər]	: that used to have a particular position or status in the past
☐ engineer	[ˌendʒɪˈnɪr]	: a person whose job involves designing and building engines, machines, roads, bridges, etc.
☐ designer	[dɪˈzaɪnər]	: a person whose job is to decide how things such as clothes, furniture, tools, etc. will look or work by making drawings, plans or patterns
☐ fire	['faɪər]	: to cause to be driven forward with force
☐ obvious	['ɑːbviəs]	: easy to see or understand

🔊 Listen and check the words ❷

ゆっくり音声[ポーズなし] 40

Listen two times to the same news read at slow speed without pauses. Check the box for each of the words and phrases below when you hear them, and write down any other information or expressions you hear.

☐ get out of hand
☐ to fire water
☐ just sounds dangerous
☐ just all kinds of things
☐ it's best not to put your hand

Notes

💡 Check your comprehension

What is the news about?

Headline

Choose the best headline for this news.

(A) World's Largest Water Gun

(B) World's Smallest Water Gun

(C) World's Most Dangerous Sound

(D) World's Largest Extinguisher

Unit 13

Check the transcript and make sure you understand the content. Then listen to the news again and again until you can catch all of it.

World's Largest Water Gun

When a former NASA engineer builds a water toy, things can get out of hand. It actually takes two hands for its designer, Mark Rober, to shoot this. It is the world's largest water pistol. It uses nitrogen gas to fire water at over—and this just sounds dangerous—430 kilometers an hour and can pressure [cut] through glass, fruit, hot dogs—just all kinds of things. Now, Rober says it's best not to put your hand in front of it, for obvious reasons.

Aired on July 20, 2018

TOEIC-style Questions

1. What did Mark Rober most recently create?
   (A) The world's largest gun
   (B) A large water pistol
   (C) A gun that shoots nitrogen gas
   (D) A hot-dog gun

2. What can one shoot through with this gun?
   (A) Fruit
   (B) Hot dogs
   (C) Glass
   (D) All of the above

Use this page to practice slash listening and shadowing. Circle the subject and underline the verb to understand subject-verb agreement.

元NASA 技術者が
「世界最強の水鉄砲」を開発

When a former NASA engineer builds a water toy, /

things can get out of hand. //

It actually takes two hands /

for its designer, Mark Rober, to shoot this. //

It is the world's largest water pistol. //

It uses nitrogen gas to fire water at over— /

and this just sounds dangerous— /

430 kilometers an hour /

and can cut through glass, fruit, hot dogs— /

just all kinds of things. //

Now, Rober says /

it's best not to put your hand in front of it, /

for obvious reasons. //

語注

water gun: 《タイトル》水鉄砲	**engineer:** 技術者、エンジニア	**get out of hand:** 手に負えなくなる、手が付けられなくなる	**nitrogen gas:** 窒素ガス
former: 元の、かつての	**build:** 〜を作り上げる、組み立てる	**take:** 〜を必要とする	**fire:** 〜を発射する、発砲する
NASA: ＝ National Aeronautics and Space Administration 米航空宇宙局	**water toy:** 水遊びのおもちゃ	**designer:** 設計者	**pressure:** 〜に圧力をかける
	things: 状況、事態	**water pistol:** 水鉄砲	**obvious:** 明らかな、明白な

■ ナチュラル音声のアクセント

オーストラリア英語

■ ニュースのミニ知識

身近にある水鉄砲でも、空気の代わりに窒素ガスを使うと、ホットドッグ、スイカ、グラスや卵などを水の威力で割ったり、切ったりすることができることを、マーク・ローバー氏は見せている。2016年に世界最大のナーフ銃、さらに、2017年に世界最大の水鉄砲がギネス世界記録に認定される一方、空気流動層（air fluidized bed）を利用した砂のプールやロケットをつけたゴルフドライバー、1日で10万個のドミノを並べるドミノロボットの発明など、マークの挑戦は続いている。

■ Technology / Engineering のミニ知識

水鉄砲でも利用されている流体工学は、機械・土木・建築・化学工学などを含む広域な技術に関連する学問分野である。例えば機械工学では、水を高速で噴射する技術は様々な分野で、加工技術として利用されている。例えば、超高圧ポンプを用いて、ウォータージェットを噴射し、原子炉の解体といった特殊作業、材料表面の洗浄、水中切断などに水は利用されている。また、土木工学の水工学は、水を利用し、水害から身を守るための様々な技術を与える。このように身近にある水は、様々な分野で研究され、利用されている。

Words & Phrases（水を使った研究開発や産業などに関連した言葉）

□ a fluid	□ 流体
□ fluid engineering	□ 流体工学
□ water jet device	□ ウォータージェット装置
□ injection pressure	□ 噴射圧力
□ hydraulic engineering	□ 水工学
□ a hydroelectric power station	□ 水力発電所
□ a hydrant	□ 消火栓
□ tap water	□ 水道水
□ river improvement; flood control	□ 治水
□ water resources	□ 水資源

■ Let's Think!

水に関わる身近な技術や研究開発を調べて、英語で（難しければ日本語で）まとめてみよう。

Listen and check the words ❶

ナチュラル音声

Listen two times to the news read at natural speed. Check the box for each of the keywords below when you hear them, and look at the definition of each word to understand the news.

		definition
☐ pill	[pɪl]	: a small flat round piece of medicine that you swallow whole, without biting it
☐ prescription	[prɪˈskrɪpʃn]	: an official piece of paper on which a doctor writes the type of medicine you should have, and which enables you to get it from a chemist's
☐ seizure	[ˈsiːʒə(r)]	: a sudden attack of an illness, especially one that affects the brain
☐ epilepsy	[ˈepɪlepsi]	: a condition affecting the nervous system that causes a person to become unconscious suddenly, often with violent movements of the body
☐ dosage	[ˈdəʊsɪdʒ]	: the amount of a medicine or drug that is taken regularly, and how often it is taken

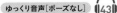 **Listen and check the words ❷**

ゆっくり音声[ポーズなし]

Listen two times to the same news read at slow speed without pauses. Check the box for each of the words and phrases below when you hear them, and write down any other information or expressions you hear.

	Notes
☐ for the first time	
☐ that's right	
☐ in people with epilepsy	
☐ a high dosage of the drug	
☐ expected to become available	

 Check your comprehension

What is the news about?

Headline

Choose the best headline for this news.

(A) The U.S. Food and Drug Manufactures

(B) The U.S. Food and Drug Administration

(C) FDA Approves 3D-Printed Figure

(D) FDA Approves 3D-Printed Pill

Check the transcript and make sure you understand the content. Then listen to the news again and again until you can catch all of it.

FDA Approves 3D-Printed Pill

Well, for the first time in history, the U.S. Food and Drug Administration has said yes to a 3D-printed pill. Yes, that's right, a pill—a prescription drug used to treat some types of seizures in people with epilepsy. Now, its manufacturer says the printing technique delivers a high dosage of the drug that is fast-dissolving and it gives them a lot more control over what goes where in the pill. It comes prepackaged in individual, premeasured doses, expected to become available early next year.

Aired on August 5, 2015

TOEIC-style Questions

1. How is this pill innovative?
   (A) It is the first drug for epilepsy.
   (B) It is a home delivery medicine.
   (C) It is a 3D-printed pill.
   (D) It is a high-dosage medication.

2. What is one advantage of this production method?
   (A) It allows more control.
   (B) It is cheap.
   (C) It uses conventional technology.
   (D) It is fast.

Use this page to practice slash listening and shadowing.
Circle the subject and underline the verb to understand
subject-verb agreement.

3Dプリンターで製造した薬を
米当局が初認可

Well, for the first time in history, /
the U.S. Food and Drug Administration has said yes /
to a 3D-printed pill. //
Yes, that's right, a pill—/
a prescription drug used to treat some types of seizures /
in people with epilepsy. //
Now, its manufacturer says /
the printing technique delivers a high dosage of the drug /
that is fast-dissolving /
and it gives them a lot more control /
over what goes where in the pill. //
It comes prepackaged in individual, premeasured doses, /
expected to become available early next year. //

語注

FDA: 《タイトル》＝ the U.S. Food and Drug Administration 米食品医薬品局	**prescription drug:** 処方薬	**manufacturer:** 製造会社、メーカー	**come:** 〜の状態で売られる
approve: 《タイトル》〜を承認する、認可する	**treat:** 〜を治療する、手当てする	**deliver:** 〜を届ける、供給する	**premeasured:** 前もって量られた
	seizure: 発作、発病	**dosage:** 1回分の投薬量、服用量	**dose:** 服用量の1回分
	epilepsy: てんかん	**fast-dissolving:** 速く溶ける、速溶性の	**(be) expected to do:** 〜する見込みである

Unit 14

■ ナチュラル音声のアクセント

オーストラリア英語

■ ニュースのミニ知識

米アプレシア製薬は、2015年8月に米食品医薬品局（FDA）が3Dプリンターで製造した薬を世界で初めて認可したと発表した。認可されたのは、同社が開発した「スプリタム」という、てんかんの発作を抑えるために使われる薬である。最高経営責任者ドン・ウェザーホールド氏によれば、この薬は、患者の薬を服用する方法を変えようとした試みからできた中枢神経系の薬で、3Dプリントの技術で、粉末状の原薬と液体を幾重にも重ねることで、舌の上で溶けやすくし、精密な用量調整をして薬の服用が困難な患者には薬を飲みやすくさせる。米国には約340万人のてんかん患者がおり、薬を飲み込むのが困難な子どもや高齢者には朗報である。

■ Science / Technology / Engineering のミニ知識

3Dプリント技術は、様々なものづくりに利用されている。この技術は、医療の分野ではオーダーメイド医療として薬、補聴器、人工骨や皮膚などの製造、航空・宇宙の分野では、エンジンの部品や燃料ノズルといった金属部品の製造、宇宙船や宇宙服の製造、また、土木・建築の分野では、プレゼンテーション用のモックアップ、プロトタイプ作成、建築模型などにも使われている。3Dプリンターは食品作りや趣味のフィギュアといった樹脂材料を利用した身近なものづくりなどにも幅広い用途で利用され、さらなる研究の余地がある。

Words & Phrases（3Dプリント技術を使った研究開発や産業などに関連した言葉）

□ inkjet printing techniques	□ インクジェット印刷技術
□ 3D food printer	□ 3D フードプリンター
□ 3D bio-printing technology	□ 3D バイオプリンティング技術
□ 3D modeling	□ 立体造形
□ rapid prototyping	□ 高速試作
□ biomedical sciences	□ 生体医学
□ hearing aid	□ 補聴器
□ artificial bone	□ 人工骨
□ computer-aided design（CAD）	□ コンピューター援用のデザイン［設計］
□ resin material	□ 樹脂材料

■ Let's Think!

3Dプリンターに関わる身近な技術や研究開発を調べて、英語で（難しければ日本語で）まとめてみよう。

◁))) Listen and check the words ❶

ナチュラル音声

Listen two times to the news read at natural speed. Check the box for each of the keywords below when you hear them, and look at the definition of each word to understand the news.

		definition
☐ brawl	[brɔːl]	: a noisy and violent fight involving a group of people, usually in a public place
☐ mill	[mɪl]	: a factory that produces a particular type of material
☐ bash	[bæʃ]	: to hit somebody/something very hard
☐ bot	[bɒt]	: a robot
☐ showdown	[ˈʃəʊdaʊn]	: an argument, a fight or a test that will settle a disagreement that has lasted for a long time

◁))) Listen and check the words ❷

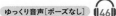

Listen two times to the same news read at slow speed without pauses. Check the box for each of the words and phrases below when you hear them, and write down any other information or expressions you hear.

	Notes
☐ went head-to-head	
☐ faced off	
☐ whipped out a chainsaw	
☐ for a finishing blow	
☐ have been waiting for	

Check your comprehension

What is the news about?

Headline

Choose the best headline for this news.

(A) Two Giant Fighting Robots in USA

(B) An Abandoned Steel Mill in Japan

(C) Japan Beats USA in Robot Fight

(D) USA Beats Japan in Robot Fight

Unit 15

Check the transcript and make sure you understand the content. Then listen to the news again and again until you can catch all of it.

USA Beats Japan in Robot Fight

Two pilots, two giant fighting machines and one massive robot brawl—the U.S. company MegaBots and Japan's Suidobashi finally went head-to-head in the battle of the century. The two piloted robots—they faced off in an abandoned steel mill in Japan, bashing cars, firing pellets, throwing punches. The brawl ended when Team USA whipped out a chainsaw for a finishing blow on the Japanese bot. Yep, that would do it. Now, fans have been waiting for the showdown for two years, ever since MegaBots issued the challenge.

Aired on October 19, 2017

TOEIC-style Questions

1. Where did this battle take place?

(A) In an abandoned factory

(B) In the United States

(C) At a fictional place in cyberspace

(D) At a secret location

2. Who or what were the contestants?

(A) Two Japanese robots

(B) Computers

(C) Fighting machines operated by pilots

(D) Video-game players

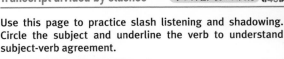

ゆっくり音声［ポーズ入り］ 🎧 45

Use this page to practice slash listening and shadowing. Circle the subject and underline the verb to understand subject-verb agreement.

リアル巨大ロボット、日米大決戦！

Two pilots, two giant fighting machines and one massive robot brawl—/

the U.S. company MegaBots and Japan's Suidobashi/

finally went head-to-head in the battle of the century.//

The two piloted robots—/

they faced off in an abandoned steel mill in Japan,/

bashing cars, firing pellets, throwing punches.//

The brawl ended/

when Team USA whipped out a chainsaw for a finishing blow on the Japanese bot.//

Yep, that would do it.//

Now, fans have been waiting for the showdown for two years,/

ever since MegaBots issued the challenge.//

語注

beat:《タイトル》～を打ち負かす、やっつける	**piloted:** 有人の、操縦者搭乗の	**bash:** ～を強くたたく、たたき壊す	**finishing blow:** とどめの一撃、一発
massive: 大がかりな、大規模な	**face off:** にらみ合う、対決する	**fire:** ～を発射する、撃つ	**bot:** ロボット
brawl: 騒々しいけんか、乱闘	**abandoned:** 放棄された、使われなくなった	**throw a punch:** 一発殴る	**showdown:** （最終的な）決着の場、対決
go head-to-head: 直接対決する	**steel mill:** 製鋼所、鉄工所	**whip out:** ～をさっと取り出す	**issue a challenge:** 挑戦状を送る

Unit 15

■ ナチュラル音声のアクセント

アメリカ英語

■ ニュースのミニ知識

水道橋重工の最高経営責任者で、造形作家の倉田光吾郎氏とロボット制御ソフト開発者である吉崎航氏らによる制作プロジェクトチームが作成した「クラタス」に、2015年アメリカメガボット社が対決の挑戦を申し出て、2017年夏にその戦いが実現した。戦いは、ロボットがノックアウトか使用不能、またはパイロットが降参するかで勝敗が決まる。油圧駆動で一撃必殺の腕を持った「クラタス」に、ミサイルランチャー搭載の「メガボット マーク2」（アイアン・グローリー）とチェーンソー搭載の「メガボット マーク3」（イーグル・プライム）が戦いを挑んだ。勝敗は1勝1敗となった。その後、「クラタス」はアマゾンで販売された（現在入手できない）。一方、「アイアン・グローリー」の3D CADデザインは25ドルで販売された。残念ながら、メガボット社は2019年に資産を清算してしまった。

■ Technology / Engineering / Arts のミニ知識

トランスフォーマーのような巨大変形ロボットから人体に入り込むナノロボットまで、アニメや映画の世界のロボットが現実に出現したらどうなるか。現在ナノロボットは、医療産業で使用が急速に見込まれ、遺伝子治療、がん治療、歯科治療などへの応用が期待されている。一方、既に、物流、製造、インフラ、家庭では仕分け、組み立て、保守点検、お掃除などを行うロボットが存在する。半世紀前に「ドラえもん」が描いた未来の世界が現実となっているものもある。巨大変形ロボットの実現はまだないが、アニメや映画で見た世界は技術の進歩と共に実現できるかもしれない。

Words & Phrases（アニメ・映画ロボットに関する研究開発や産業などに関連した言葉）
....

- □ transforming robot
- □ domestic robot
- □ nanorobot
- □ nanotechnology
- □ hydraulic drive
- □ animation
- □ science fiction film
- □ fantasy film
- □ cartoonist
- □ comic magazine

- □ 変形ロボット
- □ 家庭用ロボット
- □ ナノロボット
- □ ナノテクノロジー
- □ 油圧駆動
- □ アニメ
- □ SF 映画
- □ ファンタジー映画
- □ 漫画家
- □ 漫画雑誌

■ Let's Think!

アニメや映画に登場する技術や研究開発を調べて、英語で（難しければ日本語で）まとめてみよう。

※次ページの記事はMathematics（数学）に関する記事です。

他の章のように30秒程の長さのニュースではなく、470 words前後のリーディング記事

になりますが、STEAM教育を理解する上では興味深い内容になっています。

語注を参考にしながら読んでみましょう。

No Basis for Bias

「女子は数学が不得意」は誤り 計算中の脳の活動は男女で同等と判明

Several studies have already debunked the myth/ that boys are innately better at math than girls,/ but those are largely based on analysis of test scores.// Now, researchers also have brain imaging/ that proves young children use the same brain mechanisms and networks to solve math problems/ regardless of their gender.// The study was published in the journal *npj Science of Learning*.//

"We'd already studied the behavior of young girls and boys on mathematics tests,/ and we'd observed that their performance was statistically equivalent;/ they were indistinguishable.// They'd developed the same abilities at the same rates in early childhood,"/ said Jessica Cantlon, a professor of developmental neuroscience at Carnegie Mellon University and the study's senior author.// "But there was this lingering question of what's going on under the hood.// Is it the same neural mechanism/ that allows them to accomplish this equivalent behavior?"//

basis: 根拠	**be based on:** 〜に基づいている	**statistically:** 統計的に	**under the hood:** 中で、内部で
bias: 偏見	**analysis:** 分析	**equivalent:** 等しい、同等の	**neural mechanism:** 神経メカニズム
debunk: （通説などの）誤りを暴く、（主張などの）事実誤認を証明する	**brain imaging:** 脳撮像	**indistinguishable:** 区別がつかない	**allow...to do:** …が〜するのを可能にする
	gender: 性別	**developmental neuroscience:** 発達神経科学	**accomplish:** 〜を成し遂げる、達成する
myth: 誤った通説	**behavior:** 行動	**senior author:** 主導著者	
innately: 先天的に	**observe that:** 〜ということに気づく	**lingering:** 長引く、なかなか消えない	
math: ＝mathematics 数学	**performance:** 成績、出来栄え		

To answer this question,/ Cantlon and her team got 104 kids between the ages of 3 and 10 to take cognitive tests and watch videos of engaging math lessons/ while in an MRI scanner.// It's the first study to use neuroimaging/ to evaluate biological gender differences in the math aptitude of young children.//

"We looked at which areas of the brain responded more strongly to the mathematics content in the videos and tasks/ compared to nonmath content like reading or the alphabet.// You can define the math network by thus looking at regions that respond more strongly,"/ she said.//

"When we do that in little girls,/ we see a particular network of the brain respond,/ and when we do the same analysis in boys,/ we see the exact same regions respond.// You can overlay the network from girls on top of the network from boys,/ and they are identical,"/ she added.//

cognitive test: 認識力テスト	evaluate: 〜を査定する	task: 課題	respond: 反応する
engageing: おもしろい、興味をそそる	biological: 生物学的な	compared to: 〜と比べて	the exact same: まったく同じ
MRI scanner: 磁気共鳴診断装置	aptitude: 才能、素質、能力	define: 〜を明らかにする、明確にする	overlay A on B: AをBの上に置く
neuroimaging: 神経画像(検査)	content: 内容	region: 領域、部位	identical: まったく同じ

What Cantlon's study doesn't answer/ is why the belief that boys are stronger than girls in STEM subjects still persists.// The stereotype is so pervasive/ that one research team even felt the need to issue a consensus statement/ clarifying that "no single factor," including biology, "has been shown to determine sex differences in science and math" ability.// Cantlon said/ she thinks society and culture are likely steering girls and young women away from math and other STEM fields.//

belief: 意見、考え、所信 **STEM:** = science, technology, engineering and mathematics 科学・技術・工学・数学の教育分野の総称	**persist:** 存続する **pervasive:** 広く行きわたっている、まん延している **issue a statement:** 声明を出す	**consensus statement:** 合意声明 **clarify that:** 〜ということをはっきりさせる、明快にする **factor:** 要素、要因	**biology:** 生物学的特徴・要素 **determine:** 〜を決定する **likely:** おそらく、多分 **steer A away from B:** AをBからそらす

「女性は男性に比べ数学が苦手」は科学的に間違いであることが立証された

Cantlon pointed out/ that previous studies show that families spend more time with young boys than with young girls/ in play that involves spatial cognition,/ while teachers also preferentially spend more time with boys/ during math class.// She also noted/ that children often pick up on cues from their parents/ regarding expectations for math ability.//

"Typical socialization can exacerbate small differences between boys and girls/ so that they snowball into larger differences in how we treat them in science and math,"/ Cantlon said.// "We need to be cognizant of these origins/ to ensure we aren't the ones causing the gender inequities."//

(473 words)

previous: 以前の	note that: 〜ということを指摘する	typical: 典型的な	be cognizant of: 〜を認識する
involve: 〜を伴う、〜に関連する	pick up on: 〜に気づく	socialization: 社会化	origin: 発端、原因
spatial cognition: 空間認識	cue: （行動の）手がかり	exacerbate: （すでによくないことを）さらに悪化させる	ensure(that): 〜ということを確実にする、保証する
preferentially: 優先的に	expectation: 予想、見込み	snowball into: 雪だるま式に〜になる	inequity: 不公平、不平等

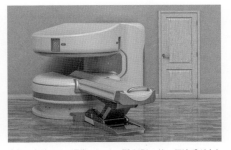

今回の実験では、通常のトンネル型 MRI に比べ圧迫感が少ないオープン型MRIが用いられた

大学生のための
CNN ニュース・リスニング：STEAM 教育編

2023 年 1 月 31 日　初版第 1 刷発行

編著者	川﨑 和基
発行者	小川 洋一郎
発行所	株式会社 朝日出版社
	〒101-0065 東京都千代田区西神田 3-3-5
	TEL：03-3239-0271　FAX：03-3239-0479
	E-MAIL：text-e@asahipress.com
	https://www.asahipress.com/
印刷・製本	錦明印刷株式会社
DTP	有限会社 ファースト
音声編集	ELEC（一般財団法人 英語教育協議会）
装丁	大下 賢一郎

©Asahi Press, 2023 All Rights Reserved. Printed in Japan ISBN978-4-255-15705-4 C1082
CNN name, logo and all associated elements TM & © 2023 Cable News Network.
A WarnerMedia Company. All Rights Reserved.

生きた英語でリスニング!

1本30秒だから、聞きやすい!

CNN
ニュース・リスニング

2022［春夏］ 電子書籍版付き
ダウンロード方式で提供

［30秒×3回聞き］方式で
世界標準の英語がだれでも聞き取れる!

- 羽生結弦、「氷上の王子」の座はゆずらない
- オックスフォード英語辞典にKカルチャー旋風
- 「母語」と「外国語」を犬も聞き分けている!…など

MP3音声・電子書籍版付き
（ダウンロード方式）
A5判 定価1100円（税込）

初級者からのニュース・リスニング

CNN
Student News

2022 夏秋

音声アプリ+動画で、どんどん聞き取れる!

- レベル別に2種類の速度の音声を収録
- ニュース動画を字幕あり/なしで視聴できる

MP3・電子書籍版・
動画付き［オンライン提供］
A5判 定価1,320円（税込）

朝日出版社 〒101-0065 東京都千代田区西神田3-3-5 TEL 03-3263-3321